LAST CALL

a cumulative guide to

MOCKTAILS

created and written by

JACK TINDLE
a.k.a The Teenage Bartender

Copyright © 2025 by Jack Tindle

ISBN: 978-1-967257-02-7 First Edition, Hardback
ISBN: 978-1-967257-15-7 Ebook
978-1-967257-08-9 Indie Bookstore Special Edition

All rights reserved.

No portion of this book may be reproduced in any form without written permission from the publisher or author, except as permitted by U.S. copyright law.

Book design by Branch and Willow Design Co.

Printed in the United States of America

1st Edition 2025

Library of Congress Control Number: 2025945061

Edit by Jon Allen

For permissions or inquiries, please contact hello@booksbyjac.com.

I'd like to say a huge thanks to both my mom and dad for always supporting my new ideas no matter how crazy they are. I'm so lucky to have you both and I can confidently say I wouldn't be where I am today without you.

I'd also like to thank my grandparents. Your unconditional love and support has given me the motivation to keep pushing to be the best version of myself.

Another huge thank you to my friend Noah. You've stuck with me through thick and thin and have always been there to support me.

To a coworker who I consider to be not just a mentor but also a friend; I'd like to extend my deepest thanks. Teodor, you've not only helped me with ideas for several of the drinks in this book, but you've also taught me what it means to be a truly great bartender/mixologist.

I'd like to extend a massive thank you to all my social media followers. Your constant support and kind words of encouragement are the reason I keep making videos and decided to write a second book in the first place.

And finally, a special thank you to:
Alexis P, Sara H, Brandi G, Aunt Annie, Jon A, Kristin C, and Mike T.
You all have helped me in your own special way throughout the years.
Your support and kindness mean the world to me!

Table of Contents

INSPIRED NON-ALCOHOLIC RECIPES

1 - 2 Introduction	23 - 24 Macadamia-Nut Espresso Martini	43 - 44 Paloma
3 - 4 Espresso Martini		45 - 46 Jungle Bird
5 - 6 French Tart	25 - 26 Manhattan	47 - 48 New York Sour
7 - 8 Botanical Beach	27 - 28 Easy Mojito	49 - 50 Clover Club
9 - 10 Extra Kick Mexican Mule	29 - 30 Elevated Mojito	51 - 52 Watermelon Mojito
11 - 12 Easy Sangria	31 - 32 Apple Mimosa	53 - 54 Easy Aperol Spritz
13 - 14 Elevated Sangria	33 - 34 Yugeño	55 - 56 Elevated Aperol Spritz
15 - 16 Midori Sour	35 - 36 Kiwi 75	57 - 58 Enzoni Sbagliato
17 - 18 Negroni	37 - 38 French Martini	59 - 60 Spicy Cucumber Mule
19 - 20 Bloody Mary	39 - 40 Sloe Berry Fizz	61 - 62 Peach Bourbon Smash
21 - 22 Spicy Bloody Mary	41 - 42 Cucumber Mojito	

MARGARITA NON-ALCOHOLIC RECIPES

63 - 64 Introduction	75 - 76 Passion Fruit Margarita
65 - 66 Kiwi Margarita	77 - 78 Pomegranate Margarita
67 - 68 Blueberry Margarita	79 - 80 Guava Margarita
69 - 70 Raspberry Margarita	81 - 82 Pineapple Margarita
71 - 72 Peach Margarita	83 - 84 Banana Margarita
73 - 74 Spicy Margarita	

Table of Contents

DESSERT NON-ALCOHOLIC RECIPES

85 - 86 Introduction	97 - 98 Butterscotch Apple
87 - 88 Creme Brule	99 - 100 Bushwacker
89 - 90 Almond Joy	101 - 102 Brian's Banana Foster
91 - 92 Peanut Butter Martini	103 - 104 Peaches and Cream
93 - 94 Butterscotch Beer	105 - 106 Dirty Banana
95 - 96 Thin Mint Martini	

ORIGINAL NON-ALCOHOLIC RECIPES

107 - 108 Introduction	125 - 126 Velvet Lex	143 - 144 Coco Bloom
109 - 110 Sweet Blue Haze	127 - 128 Liquid Limerence	145 - 146 Carmine Coppice
111 - 112 Yuzu Garden	129 - 130 Black-Berry-Cherry Spritz	147 - 148 Anise Reverie
113 - 114 Green Meadow Mist	131 - 132 Autumn Ginger	149 - 150 Desert Silk
115 - 116 Mom's Blueberry Grove	133 - 134 Agave Punch No. 3	151 - 152 Michigan Blazing Orchard
117 - 118 Coco-Noah	135 - 136 Pear Blossom Fizz	
119 - 120 Apricot Daydream	137 - 138 Fire in the Dark	153 - 154 Peach Please
121 - 122 Fizz De Violette	139 - 140 Peach Meadow	155 - 156 Crimson Cascade
123 - 124 Sippin' Sage	141 - 142 Lychee Whisper	157 - 158 The Last Sip

Table of Contents

MOCKTAIL INGREDIENT RECIPES

159 - 160	Introduction	165	Honey Syrup
161	Demerara Syrup	166	Habanero Syrup
162	Green Apple Extract	167	Cucumber Extract
163	20% Saline Solution	168	Caramel Butterscotch Cream
164	Rosemary Syrup		

TALES OF THE TEENAGE BARTENDER

169 - 170	Introduction	175	High Standards
171	$5 for a Hug	176	Side Hussle
172	Unique Palette	177 - 178	Strange Drink Orders
173	Juice Cannon	179 - 180	Most Entertaining Pick-Up Lines
174	Oh Snap!		

TIME TO GET YOUR CREATIVE JUICES FLOWING

181 - 182	Introduction	183 - 186	Blank Recipe Pages

Hello!

Thank you so much for supporting my love of mocktail making by purchasing my book. It means the world to me!

I can say with complete sincerity that this book is something I've poured my blood, sweat, and tears into. When I made the decision to write a follow-up to my first book, I knew I wanted to build on what I had already created, making something longer, more intricate, and more refined. That said, I don't really see the two books as separate works. To me, they're two halves of a bigger picture; one cohesive experience meant to grow with you.

The first book laid the foundation. It introduced the basics of mixology, covered essential tools and techniques, and offered a gradual path in recipes from beginner to intermediate to complex creations. It was meant to be a starting point, a guide to help anyone step into the world of mocktails with confidence.

This second book builds on that. It's meant for the reader who's already started experimenting and is ready to dive deeper. If the first book was about learning the ropes, this one is about letting go and running wild with everything you've learned.

Book Creation

As I mentioned earlier, I've poured (pun intended) an almost absurd amount of time, energy, and heart into creating this book. I've lost more hours of sleep over it than I can count on both hands and feet, and it consumed a huge chunk of what little free time I had. Most of this book was made while I was either attending college, working as a bartender, or at one particularly hectic point ... doing both at the same time.

Every part of this project was a labor of love. I came up with all the recipes, wrote every story and section you'll find in these pages, and even took all of the drink photos myself. Designing and building this book from the ground up was anything but easy, but I wouldn't trade the experience for anything.

Looking back now, I'm honestly amazed it all came together, but I'm even more proud of what it's become. All the long nights, creative blocks, self doubt, and chaotic moments were worth it. This book is one of the most fulfilling things I've ever made, and I hope that passion shines through in every page.

Book Tone

As you make your way through the drink descriptions, you might start to notice a familiar tone ... especially if you've ever watched my videos on social media. That was completely intentional. I wanted the writing to sound like me, like the way I talk when I'm behind the camera or chatting with a friend. It felt important that the voice throughout this book reflect who I really am, not just as a creator, but as a person.

I didn't want this to be just a collection of recipes; I wanted it to feel like a conversation wherein I guide you through your mocktail making journey. Like you're right there with me, hearing the little stories behind each drink, the emotions that inspired them, or the weird late-night ideas that somehow turned into something delicious. In that way, I feel like I've preserved a genuine piece of myself here, and that becomes more and more clear the further you read.

This book is deeply personal, even in its lightheartedness, and I hope that comes through with every page.

The Journey

Whether you know me from social media or just happened to pick this up on a whim at your local bookstore, you've probably realized by now that I also make mocktails online. What started as a fun little side project has turned into something so much bigger than I ever imagined. Between managing my social platforms and writing this book, life has been a whirlwind, in the best, most chaotic way possible.

As of writing this, I've somehow found myself with nearly 53,000 followers on Instagram, and I'm gearing up for my second appearance on WGN to talk about this very book. If you had told 16-year-old me (back when I was first experimenting with non-alcoholic drinks in my parent's kitchen) that this would be my reality, I would've laughed, rolled my eyes in disbelief, and probably asked if I was at least a professional water polo player by then.

It's honestly surreal how far this journey has come, and I'm endlessly grateful to everyone who's followed along, supported me, and shared in the excitement. I never expected any of this, but I wouldn't trade it for the world.

The Beginning

Speaking of water polo, people often ask how I got into making mocktails in the first place. I've been a little hesitant to share the full story ... but here it is. It was the summer before my junior year of high school, and my water polo future had never looked brighter. I was at the top of my game and ready for the season to start. But all that momentum came to a sudden stop when, on the very first day of practice, I broke a bone in my wrist.

With more free time than I'd had in years and no real sense of purpose, I knew I needed something to keep me grounded and pull me out of what could've easily become a downward spiral. I had played around with mocktails a bit that summer; nothing wild, just a Piña Colada and a Shirley Temple, but I really enjoyed the process and wanted to explore it more. I'd previously run a TikTok account focused on water polo, but with that off the table, I shifted gears and created a new page dedicated to mocktail making ... and just like that, The Teenage Bartender was born.

Looking back, that broken bone, which was devastating at the time, was truly a blessing in disguise.

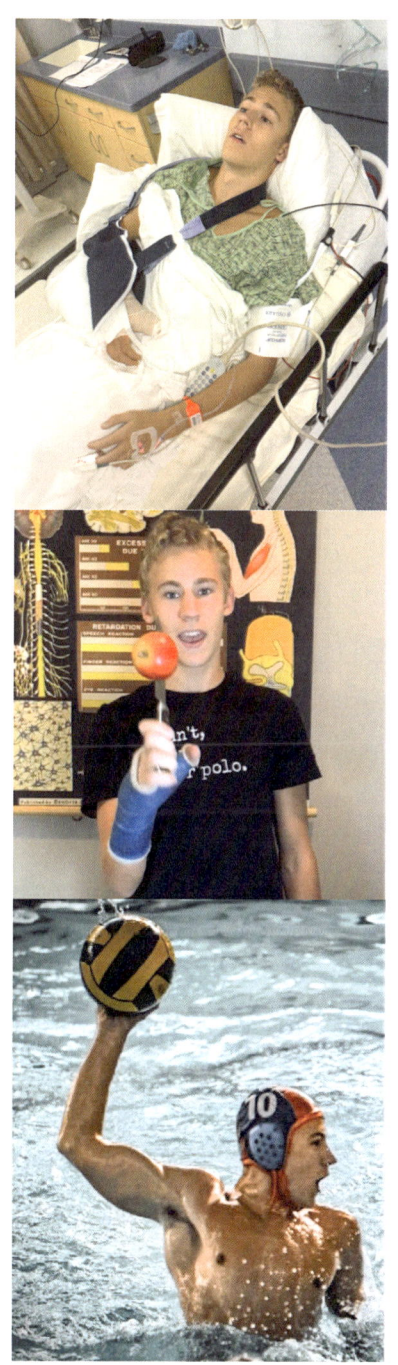

Final Remarks

I hope that throughout this little prologue of sorts, I've been able to put into words just how much passion I have for this book and for mixology as a whole. Every page, every recipe, every quirky little detail has been crafted with care, and I truly hope you enjoy exploring it all as much as I enjoyed creating it. If you've made it this far, first of all, thank you. It means a lot.

And before you dive into the drinks, I want to leave you with one final piece of advice (something I've picked up along this wild and unexpected journey): *If you're truly passionate about something, and you pour your heart and soul into it, you will see results.* Maybe not right away, and maybe not in the form you imagined … but they will come.

It might sound a little cliché, but I've found it to be deeply true. This book, and everything that led to it, is proof of that for me.

That said, I know you didn't pick this up for life advice from a teenager, so I'll get out of the way now. Enjoy the recipes, the stories, the funny quips, and all the little surprises I've tucked in along the way.

Cheers from Michigan,

The Teenage Bartender

These are drinks based on original cocktails made non-alcoholic. While I do add my own twist, the basis of the drink is in classic cocktails. I enjoy the challenge of turning a traditionally alcoholic drink into a non-alcoholic drink that's still reminiscent of the original, boasting all the same flavors while still being palatable to a general audience. So, enjoy the inspired recipes, and who knows, you might even see some drinks you've heard of before.

ESPRESSO MARTINI
NON-ALCOHOLIC

Coffee aficionados, unite! This one's for you! The espresso martini has been stealing the spotlight on social media lately, and I just knew I had to whip up my own alcohol-free twist. For those who appreciate the rich and invigorating flavor of coffee but prefer to skip the alcohol, this mocktail is a delightful alternative that doesn't compromise on taste or sophistication. Now, I know some might raise an eyebrow at using cold brew espresso instead of the traditional espresso, but trust me, it's a match made in caffeine heaven for this drink! The cold brew offers a smooth, but bold flavor that pairs beautifully with the other ingredients, creating a balanced and refreshing mocktail.

So, here's to health, wealth, and a sprinkle of happiness symbolized by the three espresso beans floated on top.

FLAVOR PROFILES:
sweet, smooth, rich

RECIPE
SINGLE SERVING

DIRECTIONS:

- Add all ingredients EXCEPT garnish into your shaker with a handful of ice.
- (Optional) Dry shake first for better foam.
- Shake vigorously with ice for 30 seconds.
- Double strain into your martini glass using a drink strainer.
- Add garnish on top.
- Take a sip of this deliciously caffeinated pick me up!

INGREDIENTS:

- 4 oz Cold Brew Espresso (I use Stok)
- 1 oz Espresso Martini Syrup
- 0.75 N/A Irish Cream Syrup
- Garnish: Three espresso beans

MARTINI GLASS

FRENCH TART
NON-ALCOHOLIC

This is one of those drinks I wasn't quite sure I'd love at first ... but wow, was I in for a pleasant surprise. Grapefruit has never really been my go-to flavor when it comes to drinks. I usually find it a bit too sharp or bitter for my taste. But with this mocktail I'm more than willing to make an exception.

What really sealed the deal for me, though, was the addition of elderflower. This was actually one of the first drinks I made using it, and it completely opened my eyes to how much depth and complexity elderflower can bring to a recipe.

Sometimes, a drink comes along and surprises you in all the best ways. It changes your mind, expanding your palate, and leaving you wondering why you hadn't tried it sooner. This one definitely did that for me.

FLAVOR PROFILES:
botanical, tart, sour

RECIPE
SINGLE SERVING

DIRECTIONS:

- Add all ingredients EXCEPT garnish into your shaker with a handful of ice.
- Shake vigorously for 30 seconds.
- Double strain into your coupe glass.
- Add your garnish on top.
- Savourez cette délicieuse boisson!

INGREDIENTS:

- 1.5 oz N/A Gin
- 2 oz Grapefruit
- 1 oz Elderflower Syrup
- 0.5 oz Lemon Juice
- Garnish: Grapefruit slice and rosemary

BOTANICAL BEACH
NON-ALCOHOLIC

Normally, you wouldn't think "botanical meets tropical" would make a match made in drink heaven, but this mocktail is here to disprove that theory. It's like a flavor fiesta in a glass, blending the herbal charm of elderflower and N/A gin with the sunny vibes of coconut and mango. It's like the tropics met a botanical garden, and they decided to throw a party … and you're invited!

The result? A symphony of tropical botanicals that'll have your taste buds dancing in a conga line. If you want to get into more herbal flavors but are a bit scared, this is a phenomenal place to start.

It's the drink equivalent of dipping your toes in the pool of bold flavors, and trust me … you'll want to dive right in.

FLAVOR PROFILES:
sweet, botanical, sour

RECIPE
SINGLE SERVING

DIRECTIONS:

- Add all ingredients EXCEPT garnish and Sprite into your shaker with a handful of ice.
- Shake vigorously for 30 seconds.
- Strain into your Collins glass using a drink strainer.
- Top with Sprite.
- Add garnish on top.
- Take a sip of this botanically tropical drink!

INGREDIENTS:

- 1.5 oz N/A Gin
- 0.75 oz Elderflower Syrup
- 1 oz Lime Juice
- 0.75 oz Cream of Coconut
- 1 oz Mango Puree
- Sprite
- Garnish: Lime wheel

EXTRA KICK MEXICAN MULE
NON-ALCOHOLIC

The original non-alcoholic Mexican Mule from my first book is a nice, refreshing drink with a bit of a spicy kick. This version ups that spicy kick to a whole new level.

The addition of "habanero lime" and ginger syrup enhances the other flavors while adding a noticeable increase in spice. It's balanced perfectly and is a great homage to the original. Now it may sound a bit intimidating with all the spicy flavors, but take it from someone who can't handle spice all that well ... it's really not that bad. It's got just enough heat to wake up your taste buds, but not burn them off. Think of it as a drink with a playful little punch ... not a knockout.

So give this one a try when you feel like spicing things up, but keep a glass of milk or a popsicle nearby, just in case.

FLAVOR PROFILES:
spicy, sweet, sour

RECIPE
SINGLE SERVING

DIRECTIONS:

- Add all ingredients EXCEPT garnish and Ginger Beer into your shaker with a handful of ice.
- Shake vigorously for 30 seconds.
- Strain into your Collins glass over ice.
- Top with ginger beer.
- Add your garnish on top.
- Enjoy with a nice side of milk!

INGREDIENTS:

- 1.5 oz N/A Tequila (Ritual for spicy effect)
- 1 oz Habanero Lime (Monnin)
- 1 oz Ginger Syrup
- 0.75 oz Lime Juice
- Ginger Beer
- Garnish: Lime wheel or habanero

EASY SANGRIA
NON-ALCOHOLIC

A Sangria at its bare bones is essentially a lot of fruit and citruses combined with wine and typically some club soda. You can adjust the sweetness, tartness, or bitterness to your liking, so there's really no wrong way to make it. This "easy" version is definitely on the sweeter side, but don't let that fool you, it still has the depth and complexity needed for a good non-alcoholic Sangria.

It's the perfect choice if you're all about that refreshing fruity, citrusy goodness.

But if you're the type who likes a little more intrigue in your glass, make sure to check out the "perfect" version on the next page.

And of course, it wouldn't be a Sangria if you didn't throw every fruit and citrus, you can find into the glass.

FLAVOR PROFILES:
sweet, tart, fruity

RECIPE
SINGLE SERVING

DIRECTIONS:

- Add all ingredients including fresh fruits and citruses into your glass.
- Stir for 30 seconds *(make sure it does not layer)*.
- Take a sip of this amalgamation of pure chaos in a glass!

INGREDIENTS:

- 3 oz Red Grape Juice
- 1.5 oz Orange Juice
- 0.5 oz Lime Juice
- 0.5 oz Raspberry Syrup
- Sprite
- Garnish: Every fresh fruit and citrus you can fit in the glass.

ROCKS GLASS

ELEVATED SANGRIA
NON-ALCOHOLIC

The non-alcoholic "easy" Sangria on the previous page was all about that sweet, citrusy punch ... like a fruit salad in a glass with a hint of sparkle. But this version? Oh, this one is stepping things up. It leans into wine's natural talent for showcasing those deep, rich notes of dark berries ... think blackberries, raspberries, and a touch of sloe berry that makes you feel like you've just walked into a lush vineyard at sunset.

The result? A beautifully complex and sophisticated blend that elevates the non-alcoholic wine to new heights and creates a beautiful drink while you're at it.

While this version is definitely less sweet than the "easy" Sangria and a bit more complicated, it more than makes up for it with layers on layers of flavor.

FLAVOR PROFILES:
sweet, rich, tart

RECIPE
SINGLE SERVING

DIRECTIONS:

- Add all ingredients including fresh fruits and citruses into your glass.
- Stir for 30 seconds *(make sure it does not layer)*.
- Take a sip of this more advanced amalgamation of pure chaos in a glass!

INGREDIENTS:

- 3 oz N/A Red Winc (not grape juice)
- 1 oz Blackberry Syrup
- 0.5 oz Lime Juice
- 0.5 oz Sloe Berry Syrup
- 0.5 oz Raspberry puree
- 3 Dashes N/A Aromatic Bitters
- Club Soda
- Garnish: Every fresh fruit and citrus you can fit in the glass.

MIDORI SOUR
NON-ALCOHOLIC

To quote a fictional horse who, back in the 90's was in a very famous TV show: "Why does Cantaloupe think every time it gets invited to a party it can bring along its dumb friend Honeydew?". But honestly, I think even he'd make an exception for this deliciously crafted non-alcoholic drink. Now, I'll admit, I'm a total sucker for sour drinks, but I didn't expect honeydew of all things to work so well with that sweet-and-sour combo.

This drink is a N/A twist on the classic Midori Sour, but with some fun changes. The first time I made it, all I had was grapefruit soda instead of lemon-lime, and it turned out to be the perfect match with the honeydew! Sweet, sour, and just a little bit unpredictable ... just the way life (and drinks) should be.

FLAVOR PROFILES:
sweet, bubbly, sour

RECIPE
SINGLE SERVING

DIRECTIONS:

- Add all ingredients EXCEPT garnish and soda into your shaker with a handful of ice.
- Shake vigorously for 30 seconds.
- Strain into your rocks glass over ice.
- Top with grapefruit soda.
- Add your garnish on top.
- Take a sip of this perfect drink that can 'dew' no wrong!

INGREDIENTS:

- 2.5 oz Honeydew Syrup
- 1 oz Lemon Juice
- 1 oz Lime Juice
- Grapefruit Soda
- Garnish: Maraschino cherries

ROCKS GLASS

NEGRONI
NON-ALCOHOLIC

Equal parts finesse, flair, and Italian perfection, the Negroni is the cocktail equivalent of a nice suit … it's classy, iconic, and just ooh la la. Think of it as an Americano's older, bolder sibling with a bit more kick. Traditionally, it's made up of equal parts booze, booze, and surprise, … more booze. But turning this into a mocktail? Now that was a bit of a liquid puzzle.

However, the result? Oh, bellissimo! It's a surprisingly delightful balance of flavors that doesn't come off too bitter.

The aromatics from the orange peel really ties everything together like a fabulous Italian scarf on a chilly day.

So, sip away! It's a taste of Italy that doesn't require a passport.

FLAVOR PROFILES:
Aromatic, botanical, bitter

RECIPE
SINGLE SERVING

DIRECTIONS:

- Add all ingredients EXCEPT garnish into a mixing glass.
- Stir ingredients with ice for 30 seconds.
- Strain into a chilled rocks glass over ice.
- Express the orange zest over the glass then rub it around the rim of the glass before placing it on top.
- Enjoy this bittersweet zesty concoction!

INGREDIENTS:

- 1.5 oz N/A Gin
- 1.5 oz N/A Campari
- 1 oz N/A Red Wine
- 0.25 oz Simple Syrup
- 2 Dashes of Aromatic Bitters
- Garnish: Orange peel

ROCKS GLASS

BLOODY MARY
NON-ALCOHOLIC

This drink is a true classic … bold, distinctive, and rooted in tradition. It's certainly not everyone's cup of tea, but those who love it tend to be die-hard fans who are convinced it's one of the greatest concoctions ever created. While I might not go quite that far, I can confidently say that my non-alcoholic Bloody Mary recipe is absolutely delicious and well worth trying. It captures all the savory depth you'd expect from the original, with rich tomato flavors layered with a carefully balanced blend of spices. Sharp, tangy notes from horseradish and dill pickle juice add an extra kick.

Now admittedly, it's a unique flavor profile that might not appeal to everyone, but for those who already appreciate a good Bloody Mary, this alcohol-free version is sure to hit the spot.

FLAVOR PROFILES:
savory, tangy, umami

RECIPE
SINGLE SERVING

DIRECTIONS:

- Add all ingredients except garnish into your Collins glass.
- Add ice to the glass.
- Stir for 30 seconds.
- Add your garnishes on top.
- Cheers from me to you!

INGREDIENTS:

- 3 oz Tomato Juice
- 0.5 oz Lemon Juice
- 0.75 oz Worcestershire Sauce
- 0.25 oz Dill Pickle Juice
- 1 Pinch Celery Salt
- 2 tsp. Horseradish
- (Optional) 1 oz N/A Beer
- Garnish: Celery stick, olives, and a pickle

SPICY BLOODY MARY
NON-ALCOHOLIC

The Bloody Mary has always gone hand in hand with spice, it's practically part of its identity. That being said, I'll admit I'm not the biggest fan of intense heat myself. My ideal non-alcoholic Bloody Mary leans more toward subtle warmth, just enough to add a little kick without stealing the show.

This recipe, however, is for the true spice enthusiasts. It delivers a vibrant, full-bodied experience with layers of tomato, citrus, and umami, all elevated by a generous punch of heat. But don't worry, the spice doesn't overpower the drink. Instead, it enhances every sip, lifting the other flavors and adding an invigorating edge.

So, if you're ready to turn up the heat without sacrificing balance, this is the bold, non-alcoholic Bloody Mary you've been waiting for.

FLAVOR PROFILES:
savory, spicy, umami

RECIPE
SINGLE SERVING

DIRECTIONS:

- Add all ingredients except garnish into your Collins glass.
- Add ice to the glass.
- Stir for 30 seconds.
- Sprinkle Tajin on top.
- Add your garnish on top.
- Sip and enjoy the spicy kick!

INGREDIENTS:

- 3 oz Tomato Juice
- 0.5 oz Habanero Lime (Monnin)
- 0.75 oz Worcestershire Sauce
- 3 dashes Tabasco Sauce
- 1 pinch Celery Salt
- (optional) 1 oz N/A Beer
- Garnish: Pepper and tajin

MACADAMIA-NUT ESPRESSO MARTINI NON-ALCOHOLIC

This drink takes everything I love from a non-alcoholic espresso martini and makes it just a bit better. I wasn't exactly a macadamia nut enthusiast before this, but when I found a bottle of macadamia syrup just lying around, I figured, "Why not use it in something." And WOW, am I glad I did! The result is a mouthwatering upgrade that gives the original espresso martini a serious run for its money.

The crushed macadamia nuts floating on top ... pure genius. They add just the right amount of salty goodness to bring this drink together like the perfect finishing touch.

It's like a cozy, nutty hug for your taste buds. A smooth, rich, and salty variation that'll have you rushing to make another in no time!

FLAVOR PROFILES:
rich, sweet, nutty

RECIPE
SINGLE SERVING

DIRECTIONS:

- Add all ingredients EXCEPT garnish into your shaker with a handful of ice.
- (Optional) Dry shake first for better foam.
- Shake vigorously for 30 seconds.
- Double strain into your martini glass using a drink strainer.
- Add garnish on top.
- Take a sip of this macada-mazing treat!

INGREDIENTS:

- 4 oz Cold Brew Espresso (I use Stok.)
- 1.5 oz Macadamia Nut Syrup (Monin)
- 1 oz Espresso Martini Syrup
- Garnish: Crushed macadamia nuts

MANHATTAN NON-ALCOHOLIC

Transforming a spirit-forward cocktail into a non-alcoholic mocktail can be like trying to find a unicorn at a petting zoo! Take the classic Manhattan, it's basically a prohibition party in a glass! The tricky part was substituting its supporting ingredient ... sweet vermouth. The sweetened fortified wine that gives the Manhattan its suave perfect balance. My genius non-alcoholic hack? Just toss in 0.75 oz of N/A red wine, 0.25 oz of simple syrup, and a couple dashes of bitters.

Boom! Suddenly, this boozy classic morphs into a savory, surprisingly balanced mocktail that everyone can sip.

And let's not forget the final touch ... a delicious Luxardo cherry for garnish. Because what's a drink without a cherry to seal the deal?

FLAVOR PROFILES:
rich, aromatic, bitter

RECIPE
SINGLE SERVING

DIRECTIONS:

- Add all ingredients EXCEPT garnish into a mixing glass.
- Stir ingredients with ice thoroughly for 30 seconds.
- Strain into a chilled coupe or martini glass.
- Add your garnish on top.
- Enjoy your non-alcoholic Manhattan ... a toast to history!

INGREDIENTS:

- 2 oz N/A Bourbon or Whiskey
- 0.75 oz N/A Red Wine
- 0.25 oz Simple Syrup
- 2-4 Dashes of Aromatic Bitters
- Garnish: Luxardo cherry

EASY MOJITO
NON-ALCOHOLIC

Mojitos are awesome ... there's no denying that minty, citrusy goodness. But let's be real, sometimes, all the fresh ingredients and muddling can feel like a bit of a hassle, especially after a long day. That's where this version comes in. I've stripped it down to the essentials, giving you all the refreshing, sweet mint flavor you crave ... without the hassle.

You've been out in the heat, you're tired, you're thirsty, and all you want is something cool, crisp, and ready in seconds. This drink is your new best friend.

BONUS: no mint leaves stuck in your teeth. It's everything you love about a mojito, minus the fuss.

So the next time you're craving an easy refreshing drink on a hot day whip one of these up!

FLAVOR PROFILES:
sweet, herbal, sour

RECIPE
SINGLE SERVING

DIRECTIONS:

- Add all ingredients EXCEPT garnish into your glass with ice.
- Stir for 30 seconds.
- Add your garnish on top.
- Savor the stress-free flavors.

INGREDIENTS:

- 2.5 oz Mojito Mix (Stirrings)
- 0.25 oz Lime Juice
- (Optional) 1 oz N/A Light Rum
- Club Soda or Lemon Lime Soda
- Garnish: Lime wheel

COLLINS GLASS

ELEVATED MOJITO
NON-ALCOHOLIC

The earlier "easy" mojito was a solid intro, but this version? It's the elevated, flavor-packed sequel that actually lives up to the hype. Using fresh lime juice, real mint, and a proper muddle unlocks essential oils and brightens every sip. No bottled shortcuts here, just real ingredients doing what they do best.

But the real game-changer is the honey syrup. Unlike plain simple syrup, honey brings a subtle depth and complexity that plays beautifully with the citrus and mint, adding a smooth, slightly floral note that lingers in the best way.

Sure, it takes a bit more time to prepare, but the result is a perfectly balanced, non-alcoholic mojito that's vibrant, refreshing, and totally worth the effort ... especially when you need a moment of calm in a glass.

FLAVOR PROFILES:
sweet, botanical, sour

RECIPE
SINGLE SERVING

DIRECTIONS:

- Muddle mint in the bottom of your glass.
- Add all ingredients EXCEPT garnish into your glass with ice.
- Stir for 30 seconds.
- Add your garnish on top.
- Enjoy this minty classic!

INGREDIENTS:

- 6-8 Mint Sprigs
- 0.75 oz Honey Syrup (recipe page 165)
- 1.5 oz Lime Juice
- (Optional) 1.5 oz N/A Light Rum
- Club Soda or Lemon Lime Soda
- Garnish: Lime wheel and mint sprig

COLLINS GLASS

APPLE MIMOSA
NON-ALCOHOLIC

Mimosas are great, I don't think anyone's arguing that. But there's always room for improvement. In the case of this non-alcoholic drink, I just had a random idea of combining apples with oranges and ran with it.

The result was a surprisingly vibrant fizzy mix that I thoroughly enjoyed. Orange can be a surprisingly overpowering flavor, so it did take quite a few iterations to find a balance between these two fruits, but the final result is a perfect mix of apples and oranges working in fruitful harmony.

So, the next time you need a fruity drink to go with your morning brunch and you wanna mix things up *(pun very much intended)* make one of these delicious drinks.

FLAVOR PROFILES:
sweet, bubbly, fresh

RECIPE
SINGLE SERVING

DIRECTIONS:

- Add all pre chilled ingredients EXCEPT garnish into your chilled glass.
- Stir for 30 seconds.
- Add your garnish on top.
- Take a sip of this fruity and fizzy brunch concoction!

INGREDIENTS:

- 1.5 oz Apple Juice (1 oz if you use cider.)
- 1.5 oz Orange Juice
- 0.5 oz N/A Triple Sec
- Sparkling Apple (Martinelli's)
- Garnish: Apple slice

YUGEÑO
NON-ALCOHOLIC

This cheeky little drink was born during my "Drinks Around the World" series, where I set out to represent Bolivia. Now, let me tell you, this one took some serious creativity! Why? Well, one of the key ingredients in the original Bolivian cocktail is Pisco, and spoiler alert, there's no easy, one-to-one substitute for that in the non-alcoholic world. But fear not! I put on my thinking cap, mixed in a little bit of magic, and voilà!

The result? A refreshingly sweet *(perhaps slightly sweeter than the original)* concoction that'll have you sipping in bliss.

I've got to be honest though, if you're looking to dial back the sugar rush, a less sweet non-alcoholic wine could work wonders. Moscato, while totally fabulous, is a dessert wine. For a lighter touch, you could opt for something a bit drier.

FLAVOR PROFILES:
sweet, citrusy, crisp

RECIPE
SINGLE SERVING

DIRECTIONS:

- Add all ingredients EXCEPT garnish into your shaker with a handful of ice.
- Shake for 30 seconds.
- Double strain into your coupe glass.
- Add your garnish on top.
- Enjoy this sweet orange concoction!

INGREDIENTS:

- 2 oz N/A Moscato
- 2.5 oz Orange Juice
- Splash of Vanilla Syrup
- (optional) 2 Dashes Aromatic Bitters
- Garnish: Orange peel and a maraschino cherry.

COUPE GLASS

KIWI 75
NON-ALCOHOLIC

If you've been following along, you know I've got a soft spot for kiwi ... it's like the underrated fruit of the drink world. Seriously, why doesn't it get more love? So, one of my personal missions this year has been to create more drinks that put kiwi in the spotlight. And, as fate would have it, this particular recipe came to me at 3 a.m. after I'd been editing videos for hours ... probably with a touch of delirium kicking in.

I've always been a fan of a classic non-alcoholic French 75, but I've often thought, "This could be just a little fruitier", and kiwi seemed like the perfect fruit to fill that void.

If you love kiwi, you've got to give this one a shot. It's bubbly, it's vibrant, and it might just become your new favorite kiwi drink too.

FLAVOR PROFILES:
sweet, sour, bubbly

RECIPE
SINGLE SERVING

DIRECTIONS:

- Add all ingredients EXCEPT garnish into your glass.
- Leave in refrigerator for 5 minutes.
- Stir for 30 seconds.
- Garnish with kiwi slice.
- Enjoy this perfectly balanced green delight!

INGREDIENTS:

- 1.5 oz N/A Gin
- 1.5 oz Kiwi Puree
- 1 oz Lemon Juice
- N/A Sparkling Brut
- Garnish: Kiwi wedge

FLUTE GLASS

FRENCH MARTINI
NON-ALCOHOLIC

As someone who spent four years immersed in French class, (oui, mon ami!) I've developed a true appreciation for a well-crafted French drink, and this one absolutely hits the mark. It's got the perfect balance: not too sweet, but just enough to keep things interesting.

I took the original recipe and swapped out the vodka for a non-alcoholic gin, which complements the raspberry and pineapple flavors beautifully. Trust me, it's a match made in drink heaven. And here's a little pro tip: if you want to take it to the next level, opt for a higher-quality raspberry puree *(I swear by Liquid Alchemist)*. It really makes a difference, adding a richer, more nuanced flavor that elevates the drink.

This isn't just a drink, it's an experience. Cheers!

FLAVOR PROFILES:
sweet, tart, botanical

RECIPE
SINGLE SERVING

DIRECTIONS:

- Muddle 3 raspberries in the bottom of your shaker.
- Add all other ingredients EXCEPT garnish into your shaker with a handful of ice.
- Shake vigorously for 30 seconds.
- Double strain into your chilled martini glass.
- Add your garnish on top.
- Enjoy this French classic.

INGREDIENTS:

- 1.5 N/A Gin
- 1.5 oz Fresh Raspberry Puree
- 3 Raspberries
- 2.5 oz Pineapple Juice
- Garnish: Lemon twist or raspberries

MARTINI GLASS

SLOE BERRY FIZZ
NON-ALCOHOLIC

Sloe berries! If you've never heard of them, they're like blackberries more mysterious tart cousin with just the right punch of sourness to make your taste buds sit up and pay attention. The only catch? These little gems are a bit elusive here in the U.S. since they're native to the U.K. But if you can track down some fresh sloe berries or grab a sloe berry syrup, you absolutely have to try this drink.

It's refreshing, delightfully sour, with a sneaky little sweetness that comes through just when you need it. It also further supports my theory that non- alcoholic gin works with any berry.

So, if you're lucky enough to get your hands on some sloe berries ... or even some syrup, give this drink a go. You won't regret it!

FLAVOR PROFILES:
sweet, botanical, sour

RECIPE
SINGLE SERVING

DIRECTIONS:

- Add all ingredients EXCEPT garnish and club soda into your shaker with a handful of ice.
- Shake vigorously for 30 seconds.
- Strain into your Collins glass over ice.
- Top with club soda.
- Add your garnish on top.
- Take a nice 'sloe' sip of this mocktail!

INGREDIENTS:

- 1.5 N/A Gin
- 1.5 oz Sloe Berry Syrup
- 1 oz Lemon Juice
- Club Soda
- Garnish: Lemon wheel or sloe berries *(If you can find them.)*

COLLINS GLASS

CUCUMBER MOJITO
NON-ALCOHOLIC

A Mojito is already one of the most refreshing drinks out there, but I set out to make it even better. And what's more refreshing than the coolest veggie around? That being Cucumbers. I threw some in a blender to make cucumber puree and let me tell you ... WOW, it's surprisingly easy to make and unbelievably refreshing. Even with just a bit of club soda it's delicious. But we're not stopping there.

For this drink I took everything I love about a non-alcoholic mojito and gave it a little extra zing.

It's the perfect sip for those scorching sunny days when you need something cool and crisp to keep you going.

Honestly, if refreshment had a name ... it would be this drink.

FLAVOR PROFILES:
refreshing, sweet, herbal

RECIPE
SINGLE SERVING

DIRECTIONS:

- Muddle mint sprigs in the shaker.
- Add all other ingredients EXCEPT garnish and soda into your shaker with a handful of ice.
- Shake vigorously for 30 seconds.
- Double strain into your Collins glass over ice.
- Top with your club soda.
- Add your ganrish on top.
- Take a sip of this refreshing cucumber delight!

INGREDIENTS:

- 1.5 oz Cucumber Extract (recipe page 167)
- 6-8 Mint Sprigs
- 1 oz Simple Syrup
- 1 oz Lime Juice
- (Optional) 1 oz N/A Light Rum
- Club soda or Lemon Lime Soda
- Garnish: Cucumber ribbon

PALOMA
NON-ALCOHOLIC

When most people think of cocktails made with grapefruit, the Paloma is often the first that comes to mind ... and for good reason. This classic Mexican drink is known for its bright, citrusy flavor and refreshing simplicity, making it a perfect choice for warm summer afternoons or evenings on the patio.

While I've kept the heart of the traditional Paloma intact, I've also introduced a few thoughtful twists to elevate the experience. Most notably, I've added a touch of habanero syrup, which brings a subtle heat that plays beautifully with the tartness of the grapefruit and the smooth agave notes in the non-alcoholic tequila. The result is a drink that's familiar and exciting.

If you're in the mood for a bold, zesty take on a beloved classic, this version of the Paloma is sure to hit the spot.

FLAVOR PROFILES:
spicy, sweet, tart

RECIPE
SINGLE SERVING

DIRECTIONS:

- Rim glass with salt using lime juice.
- Add all ingredients EXCEPT garnish and grapefruit soda into your shaker with a handful of ice.
- Shake vigorously for 30 seconds.
- Strain into your rocks glass over ice.
- Top with grapefruit soda.
- Add your garnish on top.
- Enjoy this grapefruit filled classic.

INGREDIENTS:

- 1 oz N/A Tequila
- 1.5 oz Grapefruit Juice
- 0.5 oz Lime Juice
- Grapefruit Soda
- 0.25 oz Habanero Syrup (recipe page 166)
- (Optional) 2 Dashes Grapefruit Bitters
- Salt to Rim Glass *(Preferably pink Himalayan.)*
- Garnish: Grapefruit slice

ROCKS GLASS

JUNGLE BIRD
NON-ALCOHOLIC

The first Jungle Bird cocktail originated in Malaysia in the 1970s. It was created by Jeffrey Ong for the Kuala Lumpur Hilton Hotels "Avery Bar". The Jungle Bird was served as a welcome drink to guests.

This is one of those drinks that's perfect for when you've grown tired of classic summer mocktails like the Pina Colada and Mai Tai and want to shake things up a bit. It adds some bitter blood orange notes from the non-alcoholic Campari that balance out surprisingly well with the sour pineapple, sweet and more complex demerara syrup, and non-alcoholic dark rum.

This drink definitely doesn't boast the widest appeal, but if you think you might enjoy something a bit more nuanced and complex, it's 100% worth a try.

FLAVOR PROFILES:
sweet, bitter, sour

RECIPE
SINGLE SERVING

DIRECTIONS:

- Add all ingredients EXCEPT garnish into your shaker with a handful of ice.
- Shake vigorously for 30 seconds.
- Strain into your rocks glass over ice.
- Add your garnish on top.
- Enjoy this one-of-a-kind tropical drink!

INGREDIENTS:

- 1 oz N/A Campari
- 0.5 oz Demerara Syrup (recipe page 161)
- 0.5 oz Lime Juice
- 2 oz Pineapple Juice
- (Optional) 1 oz N/A Dark Rum
- Garnish: Pineapple leaves and wedge

NEW YORK SOUR
NON-ALCOHOLIC

If a non-alcoholic Whiskey Sour is a bit too sweet for you and you want a bit more depth ... this drink is perfect for you. It's believed the original cocktail came from Chicago *(ironically)* and has undergone many name changes throughout the years.

This non-alcoholic version is a delicious tribute to the classic which is of course a tribute in its own right to the true original the Whiskey Sour.

The non-alcoholic red wine helps cut a bit of the sweetness in the drink while still balancing out quite nicely and adding some of its own unique tart flavors.

So, if you want to enjoy a beautifully layered drink that's not too sweet and deliciously tart, definitely give this a try.

FLAVOR PROFILES:
tart, savory, rich

RECIPE
SINGLE SERVING

DIRECTIONS:

- Add all ingredients EXCEPT garnish and N/A Red Wine into your shaker with a handful of ice.
- Shake vigorously for 30 seconds.
- Strain into your rocks glass over ice.
- Float your N/A red wine over a barspoon on top.
- Add your garnish on top.
- Sip on this sophisticated drink next time you want to feel like luxury.

INGREDIENTS:

- 2 oz N/A Bourbon
- 0.5 oz Demerara syrup (or 0.75 simple syrup) (recipe page 161)
- 0.75 oz Lemon Juice
- N/A Red Wine
- (Optional) 2 Dashes Aromatic Bitters
- Garnish: Lemon zest and a Luxardo cherry

ROCKS GLASS

CLOVER CLUB
NON-ALCOHOLIC

This drink is like a match made in flavor heaven, and I'm all in! Inspired by a classic cocktail that's as smooth as it is iconic, this drink is a nod to the original recipe created by the legendary Julie Reiner for her Brooklyn cocktail bar *(which, by the way, was named after the drink itself)*. But does the non-alcoholic version measure up? Oh, you bet it does!

I'll admit, my version has a bit more sweetness than the original, but don't worry, it's not a sugar overload. It's just the right amount of sweetness to balance out the tart raspberries, and paired with those crisp botanicals, it creates a drink that's beautifully sweet, tart, and refreshingly botanical all at once.

So go ahead, mix it up, and enjoy a drink that's savory and sophisticated.

FLAVOR PROFILES:
sweet, botanical, tart

RECIPE
SINGLE SERVING

DIRECTIONS:

- Add all ingredients EXCEPT garnish into your shaker with a handful of ice.
- (Optional) Dry shake first for better foam.
- Shake vigorously for 30 seconds.
- Double strain into your coupe glass.
- Add your garnish on top.
- Take a sip of this perfectly balanced raspberry delight!

INGREDIENTS:

- 1.5 oz N/A Gin
- 0.5 oz Raspberry Preserve
- 0.5 oz Raspberry Syrup
- 1 oz Lemon Juice
- 1 Egg White
- Garnish: 2 Raspberries

WATERMELON MOJITO
NON-ALCOHOLIC

Okay, okay, I know I called the N/A Cucumber Mojito the most refreshing drink of all time, but this one? This might just be its worthy rival. I whipped up this mocktail for my 'Drinks Around the World' series to represent India, where it's a popular pick. When I first tried the original recipe, I'll be honest … I was unimpressed. I almost wrote it off completely … but then, plot twist: I made some key tweaks, and now it's a full-blown refreshing masterpiece.

The sweetness from the honey blends so perfectly with the watermelon, it's like a match made in mocktail heaven. It's light, it's healthy-ish, and it's just plain delicious.

And now just writing this is making me hanker watermelon!

FLAVOR PROFILES:
herbal, sweet, fresh

RECIPE
SINGLE SERVING

DIRECTIONS:

- Muddle mint and watermelon in the bottom of your shaker.
- Add all ingredients EXCEPT garnish and soda into your shaker with a handful of ice.
- Shake vigorously for 30 seconds.
- Double strain into your Collins glass over ice.
- Top with your club soda or lemon lime soda.
- Add your garnish on top.
- Enjoy this light and refreshing concoction!

INGREDIENTS:

- 2-4 Cubes of Watermelon
- 6-8 Mint Sprigs
- 1 oz Honey Syrup (recipe page 165)
- 0.75 oz Lime Juice
- (Optional) 1 oz N/A Light Rum
- Club Soda or Lemon Lime Soda
- Garnish: Watermelon chunks and a mint sprig

COLLINS GLASS

EASY APEROL SPRITZ
NON-ALCOHOLIC

The Aperol Spritz is basically the Italian cocktail equivalent of a rockstar … everyone knows it, everyone loves it, and it's practically synonymous with summer in Italy. So naturally, I had to give the non-alcoholic version the royal treatment. After some experimenting *(and a few late-night taste tests)*, I came up with two versions, and this one is the simpler one: easier to make with more accessible ingredients and a slightly gentler palate.

Instead of diving straight into the boldness of the classic, I used sparkling grape juice, which adds a lovely sweetness and softens the edge of the aperitif. Don't worry, though; it doesn't bury the signature bitter notes of the drink. Instead, it gently balances them, letting the flavors shine without overwhelming your taste buds.

FLAVOR PROFILES:
bitter, sweet, bubbly

RECIPE
SINGLE SERVING

DIRECTIONS:

- Add all ingredients EXCEPT garnish into your glass.
- Stir for 30 seconds.
- Add your garnish in the glass.
- Take a sip of this palatable Italian masterpiece.

INGREDIENTS:

- 1.5 oz N/A Aperitif
- 1 oz N/A Orange Syrup
- 3 oz N/A Sparkling Grape Juice
- Garnish: Orange slice

ROCKS GLASS

ELEVATED APEROL SPRITZ
NON-ALCOHOLIC

Alright, let's be real. The "easy" version of this drink might have been a little more approachable, dialing down the bold bitter notes to keep things friendly. But this version? Oh, it doesn't shy away from the punch. It's got all the bold, bitter flavors you could want. I'll admit, this one was definitely a slow sipper for me, but I was hooked with each and every sip. It's like a complex puzzle for your taste buds, where each piece comes together perfectly in a burst of bold vibrant flavor.

The sparkling brut I used might still be a bit too sweet for some, in which case I would recommend a non-alcoholic prosecco, as is used in the original recipe.

It's like a little taste of la dolce vita in a glass ... what's not to love?

FLAVOR PROFILES:
bitter, sweet, bubbly

RECIPE
SINGLE SERVING

DIRECTIONS:

- Add all ingredients EXCEPT garnish into your glass.
- Stir for 30 seconds.
- Add your garnish on the glass.
- Enjoy this bold burst of citrus and bubbles!

INGREDIENTS:

- 1.5 oz N/A Aperitif
- 0.5 oz N/A Triple Sec
- 2 oz N/A Prosecco
- Garnish: Orange slice

WINE GLASS

ENZONI SBAGLIATO
NON-ALCOHOLIC

This is a non-alcoholic combination of the Negroni Sbagliato and the Enzoni, which is, in its own right, a variation on the classic Negroni, blending sophistication with a refreshing twist. I love the non-alcoholic Enzoni so much I included it in my last book and figured that adding some extra fizz could only make it better ... and I was right.

There's a perfect balance of sweet, bitter, and fizzy going on here that makes every sip feel carefully composed and thoughtfully layered. It's light, yet complex, and the non-alcoholic Campari isn't overpowering like I was worried it might be.

If you're looking for a complex, nuanced, and fizzy drink, look no further ... this is it. A drink that manages to feel both playful and grown-up at the same time.

FLAVOR PROFILES:
bitter, bubbly crisp

RECIPE
SINGLE SERVING

DIRECTIONS:

- Muddle grapes in the bottom of the mixing glass.
- Add all other ingredients EXCEPT garnish and N/A Prosecco into your mixing glass with ice.
- Stir for 30 seconds.
- Double strain into your rocks glass over ice.
- Top with your N/A Prosecco.
- Add your garnish on top.
- Enjoy this delightfully bubbly combination!

INGREDIENTS:

- 1 oz N/A Campari
- 0.25 oz Simple Syrup
- 3 Large Green Grapes
- 2 oz N/A Prosecco
- Garnish: A green grape sliced in half on a garnish pick.

ROCKS GLASS

SPICY CUCUMBER MULE
NON-ALCOHOLIC

This drink is actually based on an alcoholic cocktail I used to make back at one of my previous jobs. I thought the idea to balance crisp, cooling cucumber with the subtle heat of habanero and the bold, zesty bite of ginger was nothing short of phenomenal, and I knew right away I had to try making a non-alcoholic version that still captured that same punchy spirit. The end result is both spicy and refreshing.

As someone who isn't typically a huge fan of overly spicy things, I was pleasantly surprised to find that the heat here is mild enough to manage, but still strong enough to give a satisfying kick that makes the drink feel exciting.

Overall, this drink is perfect for people who love ginger, enjoy a bit of heat, and want something bold and memorable without the alcohol.

FLAVOR PROFILES:
spicy, bubbly, sweet

RECIPE
SINGLE SERVING

DIRECTIONS:

- Add all ingredients EXCEPT garnish and Ginger Beer into your mixing glass with ice.
- Stir for 30 seconds.
- Strain into your mule mug over ice.
- Top with ginger beer.
- Add your garnish on top.
- Enjoy this mix of heat and coolness!

INGREDIENTS:

- 1 oz Habanero Lime (Monin)
- 1.5 oz Cucumber Extract (recipe page 167)
- 0.25 oz Ginger Syrup
- 0.5 oz Honey Syrup
- Ginger Beer
- Garnish: Cucumber slice

COPPER MULE MUG

PEACH BOURBON SMASH
NON-ALCOHOLIC

Let's be real ... peaches are delicious. But put them into a drink, and now we're talking next-level goodness. This mocktail is no exception, and for a long time, it was my answer whenever anyone asked me for my favorite drink. Sweet, juicy peach, and the herbal kick of mint come together in perfect harmony, creating a flavor that's truly one-of-a-kind. I honestly haven't found anything else like it.

A little bonus: this was one of the three drinks I created for an event with the Association of Food and Drug Officials, and it's been one of my go-to favorites ever since. Something about the cool mint and sweet peach is truly addicting.

It's the kind of drink you want to sip slowly and savor ... honestly, I don't think I'll ever get tired of it.

FLAVOR PROFILES:
herbal, sweet, sour

RECIPE
SINGLE SERVING

DIRECTIONS:

- Muddle fresh mint sprigs in the bottom of your shaker.
- Add all ingredients EXCEPT garnish and soda into your shaker with a handful of ice.
- Shake vigorously for 30 seconds.
- Strain into your rocks glass over ice.
- Top with club soda.
- Add your garnish on top.
- Enjoy the refreshing peach flavors!

INGREDIENTS:

- 1.5 oz N/A Bourbon
- 1 oz Peach Puree
- 0.5 oz Lemon Juice
- 0.5 oz Cinnamon Sugar Syrup
- 3-4 Mint Sprigs
- Club Soda
- Garnish: Mint sprig and a peach slice.

Today we will be making a...

MARGARITA

mocktail

Mondays are associated with many things ... most of which are less than positive. The start of a long week of work and the end of a relaxing weekend. I found myself in the same cycle dreading each Monday until I decided to start a new series on social media ... *Non-Alcoholic Margarita Monday*. Each Monday I made a new non-alcoholic margarita. The series caught on and I ended up making some absolutely delicious non-alcoholic margaritas. The ten recipes you're about to experience are some of my favorites. Enjoy!

KIWI MARGARITA
NON-ALCOHOLIC

If you've read any of the "kiwi recipes" up to this point, you've probably figured out that I'm a huge fan of the green berry *(yes kiwi's technically a berry)*. It's beautifully complex, and when paired with the right combination of flavors, it really shines. And this drink? It does just that ... highlighting the kiwi in a way that's totally unique.

I'm tempted to call this a non-alcoholic "Spicy Kiwi Margarita" because it uses Ritual's non-alcoholic tequila, which brings in some jalapeños.

I know, I know, it might sound a little intimidating to some, but let me reassure you *(from someone who doesn't usually love spice)* it creates the perfect subtle burn. That heat balances so wonderfully with the bright, tangy kiwi, making each sip an exciting flavor journey.

FLAVOR PROFILES:
sour, savory, sweet

RECIPE
SINGLE SERVING

DIRECTIONS:

- Add all ingredients EXCEPT garnish into your shaker with a handful of ice.
- Shake vigorously for 30 seconds.
- Open pour into your margarita glass.
- Add your garnish on top.
- Savor this bright beautiful drink!

INGREDIENTS:

- 1.5 oz Kiwi Puree
- 0.5 oz Agave Nectar
- (Optional) 1 oz N/A Tequila
- 1 oz Fresh Lime Juice
- 0.75 oz N/A Triple Sec
- Garnish: Kiwi slice

MARGARITA GLASS

BLUEBERRY MARGARITA
NON-ALCOHOLIC

Blueberries + sour drinks = a match made in flavor heaven! And what drink is more famous for its bold sour kick than the Margarita? So naturally, I had to whip up a non-alcoholic Blueberry Margarita … because, why not? The result? Pure magic! Not only is it packed with vibrant, mouthwatering flavor, but it also comes with a gorgeous color that practically screams blueberry as it sits in your glass.

If you're a fan of blueberries *(or really, just sweet and sour drinks in general)*, this one is a total game-changer. It's the perfect balance of tart and fruity, with just the right amount of zest.

So go ahead, pour yourself a glass of this beautiful drink and let the blueberry magic work its charm!

FLAVOR PROFILES:
sour, tart, sweet

RECIPE
SINGLE SERVING

DIRECTIONS:

- Add all ingredients EXCEPT garnish into your shaker with a handful of ice.
- Shake vigorously for 30 seconds.
- Open pour into your margarita glass.
- Add your garnish on top.
- Take a sip of this blueberry beverage!

INGREDIENTS:

- 1 oz Blueberry Syrup
- 0.5 oz Blueberry Puree/Jam
- 0.5 oz Agave Nectar
- (Optional) 1 oz N/A Tequila
- 1 oz Fresh Lime Juice
- 0.75 oz N/A Triple Sec
- Garnish: Blueberries or lime wheel

MARGARITA GLASS

RASPBERRY MARGARITA
NON-ALCOHOLIC

Raspberry is one of those magical fruits that somehow manages to do it all ... it's a little bit sour, a little bit sweet, and can even bring a nice tart punch to any drink. So, when I set out to make this non-alcoholic Margarita, I knew I had a ton of possibilities to work with. But after some trial and error *(and maybe a few taste tests)*, I landed on the perfect balance.

What I ended up with is a gorgeous blend of raspberry's natural tartness, paired with the more vibrant, juicy sweet notes that bring everything together in a truly delicious way. It's the kind of drink that hits all the right spots, refreshing, fruity, and with just the right amount of zing.

Cheers to fruity raspberry perfection!

FLAVOR PROFILES:
sweet, tart, fruity

RECIPE
SINGLE SERVING

DIRECTIONS:

- Add all ingredients EXCEPT garnish into your shaker with a handful of ice.
- Shake vigorously for 30 seconds.
- Open pour into your margarita glass.
- Add your garnish on top.
- Savor this berrylicious *(I know that's not a word)* drink!

INGREDIENTS:

- 1 oz Raspberry Puree
- 0.5 oz Raspberry Syrup
- 0.5 oz Agave Nectar
- 1 oz Fresh Lime Juice
- 0.75 oz N/A Triple Sec
- (Optional) Muddle 3 Fresh Raspberries
- (Optional) 1 oz N/A Tequila
- Garnish: Lime wheel or fresh raspberries

PEACH MARGARITA
NON-ALCOHOLIC

Peach has been one of my all-time favorite flavors for years, so when I decided to throw it into a non-alcoholic Margarita, it just had to work. And guess what? The result? Pure peach perfection! The juicy, savory notes of peach blend so beautifully with the zingy, sharp sourness of lime juice ... it's like a flavor match made in Margarita heaven. Plus, that color? Absolutely stunning. The bright orange hue is like a ray of sunshine in a glass.

If you're a peach lover *(and who isn't?)*, this non-alcoholic Margarita is an absolute must-try. It's vibrant, refreshing, and bursting with flavor.

Once you try it, you'll be wondering why this combination isn't a classic. Trust me, this is one sip you won't forget.

FLAVOR PROFILES:
sour, savory, bright

RECIPE
SINGLE SERVING

DIRECTIONS:

- Add all ingredients EXCEPT garnish into your shaker with a handful of ice.
- Shake vigorously for 30 seconds.
- Open pour into your margarita glass.
- Add your garnish on top.
- Enjoy this vibrant splash of deliciousness!

INGREDIENTS:

- 1.5 oz Peach Puree
- 0.5 oz Agave Nectar
- 1 oz Fresh Lime Juice
- 0.75 oz N/A Triple Sec
- (Optional) 1 oz N/A Tequila
- Garnish: Lime wheel or fresh peach slice

MARGARITA GLASS

SPICY MARGARITA
NON-ALCOHOLIC

Full transparency: I'm not usually a fan of spicy foods. I'm the type of person who prefers to keep things a bit more mild and avoid anything that might leave me reaching for a glass of milk after a bite. So, you can imagine my surprise the first time I tried a spicy drink and actually enjoyed it! At first, I thought it was a wild idea, but the moment I took a sip, I realized there was something magical about the way the heat played off the other flavors.

The key, I discovered, is all about balance. Too much spice, and it overwhelms everything else. Too little, and it's just a hint of spice with no punch.

If you've been hesitant to try spicy drinks ... this one might just change your mind and palate!

FLAVOR PROFILES:
sour, spicy, sweet

RECIPE
SINGLE SERVING

DIRECTIONS:

- Rim margarita glass with Tajin.
- Add all ingredients EXCEPT garnish into your shaker with a handful of ice.
- Shake vigorously for 30 seconds.
- Open pour into your margarita glass.
- Add your garnish on top.
- Savor this sizzling sensation!

INGREDIENTS:

- 1.5 oz Habanero Lime (Monnin)
- 0.75 oz Agave Nectar
- 0.5 oz Fresh Lime Juice
- 0.75 oz N/A Triple Sec
- (Optional) 1 oz N/A Tequila (Ritual)
- Tajin
- Garnish: Lime wheel

MARGARITA GLASS

PASSION FRUIT MARGARITA
NON-ALCOHOLIC

Passion fruit has a delicious flavor profile consisting of a bright sweetness and tart acidity that works perfectly in a non-alcoholic Margarita.

It boosts the sweetness of the agave, adding gentle notes of vanilla and honey.

It also enhances the sour notes of the lime by contributing an acidity more reminiscent of pineapple, which in turn adds a subtle tropical vibe.

If you enjoy the sweet and sour notes in a classic non-alcoholic Margarita, this drink will definitely be up your alley, and there's a ton of other delicious mocktails you can use passion fruit in.

FLAVOR PROFILES:
sour, sweet savory

RECIPE
SINGLE SERVING

DIRECTIONS:

- Add all ingredients EXCEPT garnish into your shaker with a handful of ice.
- Shake vigorously for 30 seconds.
- Open pour into your margarita glass.
- Add your garnish on top.
- You'll be passionate about how much you love this one!

INGREDIENTS:

- 1.5 oz Passion Fruit Puree
- 0.5 oz Agave Nectar
- 1 oz Fresh Lime Juice
- 0.75 oz N/A Triple Sec
- (Optional) 1 oz N/A Tequila
- Garnish: Lime wheel or fresh passion fruit

MARGARITA GLASS

POMEGRANATE MARGARITA
NON-ALCOHOLIC

Pomegranate in a non-alcoholic Margarita? Yeah, I know … it doesn't exactly scream "Margarita material" at first glance. Honestly, I was right there with you. But that's the beauty of my *"Non-Alcoholic Margarita Monday"* series, it's all about stepping out of the comfort zone and trying new things. And let me tell you, I'm so glad I did! To my absolute delight, this pomegranate twist turned out to be one of the best non-alcoholic Margaritas I've ever had.

The pomegranate adds this unexpected depth, perfectly balancing the sweet and sour notes while playing beautifully with the agave.

So, if you're ready to shake up your Margarita game and try something new, trust me … this one's worth a sip!

FLAVOR PROFILES:
sour, tart, sweet

RECIPE
SINGLE SERVING

DIRECTIONS:

- Add all ingredients EXCEPT garnish into your shaker with a handful of ice.
- Shake vigorously for 30 seconds.
- Open pour into your margarita glass.
- Add your garnish on top.
- I promise you you'll love your pom-azing drink!

INGREDIENTS:

- 1.5 oz Pomegranate Juice
- 0.5 oz Agave Nectar
- 1 oz Fresh Lime Juice
- 0.75 oz N/A Triple Sec
- (Optional) 1 oz N/A Tequila
- Garnish: Lime wheel or pomegranate

GUAVA MARGARITA
NON-ALCOHOLIC

Guava has this unique tropical yet savory flavor that's surprisingly tough to incorporate into drinks. It pairs well with agave and tequila, so it made sense to try it in a non-alcoholic Margarita.

My first attempt, however, was a bit of a mess; the guava clashed with the lime's acidity and the kick from the non-alcoholic tequila really didn't help.

But after a few tweaks, I nailed the perfect balance. The result? A refreshing, *(dare I say)* tropical Margarita that hits all the right notes without the guava overpowering anything.

Definitely worth the trial and error for this delicious non-alcoholic Margarita!

FLAVOR PROFILES:
sour, earthy, savory

RECIPE
SINGLE SERVING

DIRECTIONS:

- Add all ingredients EXCEPT garnish into your shaker with a handful of ice.
- Shake vigorously for 30 seconds.
- Open pour into your margarita glass.
- Add your garnish on top.
- Enjoy the beautiful blend of sweet, sour, and savory!

INGREDIENTS:

- 1.5 oz Guava Extract
- 0.5 oz Agave Nectar
- 1 oz Fresh Lime Juice
- 0.75 oz N/A Triple Sec
- (Optional) 1 oz N/A Tequila
- Garnish: Lime wheel or fresh guava

MARGARITA GLASS

PINEAPPLE MARGARITA NON-ALCOHOLIC

I've got Jimmy Buffett to thank for forever linking the Margarita to tropical vacations. And while I'm not going to argue that a non-alcoholic Margarita on a sunny summer day sounds absolutely perfect; I wanted to take things up a notch. Enter the non-alcoholic Pineapple Margarita! I mean, pineapple is the fruit that practically begs to be paired with all kinds of tropical flavors, so why not go all in?

That said, getting the balance just right took a couple of tries. Pineapple isn't exactly an overly sweet fruit, so finding that perfect harmony of flavors was key. But trust me, the effort was absolutely worth it. The end result? A refreshing, tangy tropical Margarita that tastes like a vacation in a glass. It's everything you love about a non-alcoholic Margarita, with a little extra tropical twist.

FLAVOR PROFILES:
sour, tropical, sweet

RECIPE
SINGLE SERVING

DIRECTIONS:

- Add all ingredients EXCEPT garnish into your shaker with a handful of ice.
- Shake vigorously for 30 seconds.
- Open pour into your margarita glass.
- Add your garnish on top.
- Enjoy this tropical treat!

INGREDIENTS:

- 1.5 oz Pineapple Juice
- 0.5 oz Agave Nectar
- 1 oz Fresh Lime Juice
- 0.75 oz N/A Triple Sec
- (Optional) 1 oz N/A Tequila
- Garnish: Lime wheel or pineapple slice

MARGARITA GLASS

BANANA MARGARITA
NON-ALCOHOLIC

Full transparency: I originally whipped this up because, well, I was out of ideas for my usual "Margarita Monday" and, purely by chance, happened to have some banana syrup gathering dust in my cupboard. What was supposed to be a random experiment turned into something way ... WAY more exciting *(and a little shocking, as you can clearly see in the video where I first try this drink)*.

The real magic here is the way the savory, almost tropical notes from the banana syrup blend seamlessly with the zingy, tart citrus kick that's at the heart of every Margarita.

I could sit here for hours describing the flavor profile, but at the end of the day, the only way you'll really get
it is by trying it yourself.

FLAVOR PROFILES:
sour, sweet, savory

RECIPE
SINGLE SERVING

DIRECTIONS:

- Add all ingredients EXCEPT garnish into your shaker with a handful of ice.
- Shake vigorously for 30 seconds.
- Open pour into your margarita glass.
- Add your garnish on top.
- Enjoy this deliciously *appeeling* drink!

INGREDIENTS:

- 1.5 oz Banana Syrup
- 0.5 oz Agave Nectar
- 1 oz Fresh Lime Juice
- 0.75 oz N/A Triple Sec
- (Optional) 1 oz N/A Tequila
- Garnish: Lime wheel or banana slice

Today we will be making a...

DESSERT

mocktail

Who doesn't love a nice, sweet dessert? Certainly not me, which is probably why I hold such a special place in my heart for dessert themed drinks. They're sweet, fun, and whimsical. Palatable to most everybody and for all intensive purposes, a dessert in liquid form. The ten dessert inspired recipes you're about to experience are some of my personal favorites in not just the dessert drink category ... but in general.

CRÈME BRULÉ
NON-ALCOHOLIC

This drink was a true labor of love, and believe me, it took quite a few attempts *(and more than a little powdered sugar related chaos)* to perfect. Caramelizing a solid layer right on top of a drink is no small feat. It's part science experiment, part mixology wizardry, and every bit worth the effort.

If you're a fan of crème brulé *(and honestly, who isn't)* this drink will capture everything you love about the classic dessert: the rich vanilla custard flavor, the delicate sweetness, and of course, that crackly caramel top you get to break through with a satisfying tap.

Beneath the brulé top is a velvety, creamy concoction that's deliciously rich in flavor. It might take a little finesse to get it just right, but once you do, you'll have a creation that's equal parts impressive and irresistible.

FLAVOR PROFILES:
sweet, savory, crispy

RECIPE
SINGLE SERVING

DIRECTIONS:

- Add all ingredients EXCEPT powdered sugar into your shaker with a handful of ice.
- Shake vigorously for 30 seconds.
- Double strain into a chilled coupe glass.
- Layer powdered sugar on top.
- Light on fire to create a hard layer using a creme brulee torch.
- Crack the delicious top layer and enjoy!

INGREDIENTS:

- 2 oz Vanilla Syrup
- 1.5 oz Heavy Cream
- 0.5 oz White Chocolate Sauce
- Powdered Sugar

ALMOND JOY
NON-ALCOHOLIC

Let's be real ... Almond Joys are absolutely delicious. I don't think anyone's arguing that. You've got that perfect combo of rich, savory chocolate, creamy coconut, and of course, the satisfying crunch of the almond in the middle. It's a classic for a reason. So, I thought, why not turn all those amazing flavors into a non-alcoholic drink? And thus, the non-alcoholic Almond Joy was born.

Now, a quick disclaimer: if you have a nut allergy, this might not be the drink for you, because, well, it's all about the almonds! But if you're someone who loves the combo of almond and coconut, this is the dessert-in-a-glass you've been waiting for.

The result is a creamy, nutty, coconutty delight that tastes like the candy bar you know and love.

FLAVOR PROFILES:
sweet, nutty, creamy

RECIPE
SINGLE SERVING

DIRECTIONS:

- Add all ingredients EXCEPT garnish into your shaker with a handful of ice.
- Shake vigorously for 30 seconds.
- Double strain into a chilled Irish Coffee mug.
- Add whipped cream on top.
- Pour crushed up almonds over the whipped cream.
- A perfect substitute for the delicious almond coconut candy!

INGREDIENTS:

- 2.5 oz Orgeat
- 2 oz Cream of Coconut
- 0.75 oz Chocolate Sauce
- 1.5 oz Heavy Cream
- (Optional) 1 oz N/A Amaretto
- Garnish: Whipped cream and crushed up almonds

PEANUT BUTTER MARTINI
NON-ALCOHOLIC

I'm nuts about a particular peanut butter candy that, for legal reasons, I can't say the name of here. My goal with this drink was to create a near liquid replica of that delicious candy. And guess what? I did it! What I came up with is a decadently creamy drink that tastes just like the peanut butter candy ... but in liquid form.

The decision to use actual peanut butter? Bold move! But honestly, it's what gives this drink its rich, smooth texture and makes it irresistibly savory. In my humble opinion, it's a game-changer.

Needless to say, any peanut butter lover will relish this drink. And the best part? Once you're done sipping, you can snack on the candies that adorn the rim of your glass.

FLAVOR PROFILES:
sweet, rich, savory

RECIPE
SINGLE SERVING

DIRECTIONS:

- Rim your martini glass with the crushed up candy.
- Add all ingredients EXCEPT garnish into your shaker with a handful of ice.
- Shake vigorously for 60 seconds.
- Double strain into a chilled martini glass.
- Enjoy this delicious peanut buttery treat!

INGREDIENTS:

- 1 tsp of Peanut Butter (smoother the better)
- 1 oz Peanut Butter Syrup
- 1.5 oz Chocolate Sauce
- 1.5 oz Heavy Cream
- Garnish: Crushed up peanut butter candies on the rim.

MARTINI GLASS

BUTTERSCOTCH BEER
NON-ALCOHOLIC

For legal reasons, I can't exactly call this drink by its original name ... but let's just say it's *magical* ... and no, I'm not exaggerating. The inspiration behind this creation came from my first sip of the version at Universal, which, let's be real, is pretty good. But my version? Phenomenal!

I took that original idea and kicked it up a notch with a luscious, thick butterscotch caramel cream that sits perfectly on top, adding the kind of richness that just takes it to the next level. As someone who LOVES butterscotch, this is, without a doubt, one of my absolute favorites. It's got everything you want: sweet, creamy, indulgent, and just the right amount of magic.

Don't just take my word for it ... make it, sip it, and let the enchantment begin.

FLAVOR PROFILES:
sweet, fizzy, rich

RECIPE
SINGLE SERVING

DIRECTIONS:

- Add cream soda and butterscotch syrup to the mug 3/4 of the way, then place in a refrigerator.
- Make your Butterscotch Caramel Cream (recipe page 166).
- Layer the cream on top of the drink pouring slowly.
- Enjoy this magically delicious drink *(wink wink)*.

INGREDIENTS:

- Cream Soda
- 2.5 oz Butterscotch Syrup
- Caramel Butterscotch Cream (recipe page 168)
- (Optional) 1.5 oz N/A Amaretto

THIN MINT MARTINI
NON-ALCOHOLIC

Thin Mints are dangerously delicious ... like, "accidentally eat a whole sleeve in one sitting" delicious. So naturally, I thought: why not turn that minty-chocolate magic into something sippable? After a few delicious test runs *(and maybe a few more cookies than strictly necessary)*. This drink totally nails the essence of a Thin Mint. It's rich, complex, perfectly balanced, and basically a dessert in a glass. And just when you think it can't get better ... a generous sprinkle of crushed Thin Mint on top seals the deal.

In short, if your favorite cookie had a liquid twin, this would be it, creamy, delicious, and guaranteed to put a smile on your face. So, grab a glass, take a sip, and let the Thin Mint magic work its deliciously minty charm. You might just wonder why you haven't been drinking cookies all along.

FLAVOR PROFILES:
sweet, savory, minty

RECIPE
SINGLE SERVING

DIRECTIONS:

- Add all ingredients EXCEPT garnish into your shaker with a handful of ice.
- Shake vigorously for 30 seconds.
- Double strain into a chilled martini glass.
- Add whipped cream on top.
- Pour crushed thin mint cookies over whipped cream.
- Take a sip of this minty sweet delight!

INGREDIENTS:

- 1.5 oz N/A Creme de Menthe
- 1.5 oz Dark Chocolate Syrup
- 1.5 oz Heavy Cream
- (Optional) 0.5 oz N/A Coffee Liqueur
- Garnish: Whipped cream and crushed up Thin Mint cookies

BUTTERSCOTCH APPLE
NON-ALCOHOLIC

Caramel apples are a classic fall staple but let's be real, butterscotch might just be an upgrade to caramel. It's richer, smoother, and has that deep buttery flavor that takes everything up a notch. That was my thinking behind this drink, and surprisingly it totally worked.

This one's definitely on the sweeter side, but the combination of the creamy butterscotch and the tart kick from the sour apple syrup creates a really fun, balanced flavor. It's sweet, tangy, and just indulgent enough without going over the top.

Whether you're sipping it at a Halloween party, or just cozying up on a crisp fall evening, this drink captures the essence of the season. And if you happen to have a Caramel Apple Pop on the side? Even better. It's a playful, nostalgic twist on classic Fall flavors.

FLAVOR PROFILES:
sweet, sour, tart

RECIPE
SINGLE SERVING

DIRECTIONS:

- Add all ingredients EXCEPT garnish and Sprite into your shaker with a handful of ice.
- Shake vigorously for 30 seconds.
- Double strain into a chilled martini glass.
- Add Sprite on top.
- Add your garnish on the glass.
- Enjoy this caramel apple in a glass ... but better!

INGREDIENTS:

- 1.5 oz Butterscotch Syrup
- 1.5 oz Sour Green Apple Syrup
- 1 oz Apple Juice
- Sprite
- Garnish: Apple Slice with butterscotch sauce on it.

BUSHWACKER NON-ALCOHOLIC

This is easily one of my favorite dessert drinks. It leans more toward a milkshake than a traditional beverage, but that's part of its charm. The combination of bold coffee, rich chocolate, and creamy coconut makes for a perfectly indulgent treat that's both smooth and flavorful. It strikes a great balance: sweet and creamy, with just enough depth from the coffee to keep things interesting.

Even if you're not a huge coffee drinker, I think you'll still enjoy this. My Mom's a great example. She's never liked coffee much, but she absolutely loves this drink. It's just that good.

Whether you're winding down after a stressful day, or just in the mood for something sweet and satisfying, this one definitely hits the spot.

FLAVOR PROFILES:
sweet, creamy, rich

RECIPE
SINGLE SERVING

DIRECTIONS:

- Rim glass with coconut flakes.
- Add all ingredients EXCEPT garnish and coconut flakes into your shaker with a handful of ice.
- Shake vigorously for 30 seconds.
- Strain into a hurricane glass.
- Add your garnish on top.
- Enjoy this delightful dessert drink.

INGREDIENTS:

- 2 oz Cold-Brew Coffee
- 2 oz Chocolate Syrup
- 2 oz Cream of Coconut
- 3 oz Half and Half
- (Optional) 1 oz Coffee Syrup
- Coconut Flakes
- Garnish: Whipped cream and chocolate sauce

BRIAN'S BANANA FOSTER NON-ALCOHOLIC

I have drinks named after both my parents in this book and this one happens to be my Dad's. My Dad always helps me with my videos with everything from helping me set up my camera and lights to washing my bar equipment. So I wanted to make a truly special drink for him.

He's a big fan of bananas in drinks and more dessert themed drinks. This drink is both of those things and absolutely delicious. It imitates the iconic dessert Banana Foster with notes of sweet banana, cream, and salted caramel. The garnish being a caramel soaked and roasted banana also adds to the Banana Foster aesthetic.

It's a deliciously balanced dessert drink and serves as a tribute to one of the greatest men I know in my life ... my father.

FLAVOR PROFILES:
sweet, creamy, salty

RECIPE
SINGLE SERVING

DIRECTIONS:

- Add all ingredients EXCEPT garnish into your shaker with a handful of ice.
- Shake vigorously for 30 seconds.
- Double strain into a chilled coupe glass.
- Add your garnish on top.
- Sip this banana fueled blast in a glass!

INGREDIENTS:

- 1.5 oz Banana Syrup
- 1 oz Salted Caramel Syrup
- 1.5 oz Half and Half
- (Optional) 3 Dashes 20% Saline Solution (recipe page 163)
- Garnish: Banana slice doused in caramel and burnt with a torch.

PEACHES AND CREAM
NON-ALCOHOLIC

Peaches are often associated with more vibrant fruity flavors in drinks, but rarely with creamier sweeter dessert flavors.

I sought to change that with this drink. It's inspired by the classic combo of peaches and cream with a bit of vanilla added for extra sweetness.

The end result is absolutely delicious. The half and half adds a nice thicker texture to the drink while still enhancing the sweetness. As for the peach, it works amazingly, even without any other sour notes. Finally, the vanilla as mentioned before helps to really balance out the sweetness in the drink.

This is really just a combination you have to try for yourself, whether you're a fan of peaches or just dessert drinks in general.

FLAVOR PROFILES:
sweet, fruity, creamy

RECIPE
SINGLE SERVING

DIRECTIONS:

- Crush freeze dried peaches and rim glass with them.
- Add all ingredients EXCEPT garnish into your shaker with a handful of ice.
- Shake vigorously for 30 seconds.
- Double strain into a chilled coupe glass.
- Add your garnish on top.
- Savor this creamy peach treat!

INGREDIENTS:

- 1.5 oz Peach Puree
- 0.5 oz Peach Syrup
- 1.5 oz Half and Half
- 1 oz Vanilla Syrup
- Freeze Dried Peaches
- Garnish: Peach slice

DIRTY BANANA
NON-ALCOHOLIC

Banana ... who knew this humble fruit could be such a chameleon in drinks? It's like the ultimate versatile flavor, showing up in everything from sweet sips to tangy concoctions. And hey, I'm still dreaming of the day I try it in an herbal drink *(I'm thinking it could be a game changer!)*. But one thing's for sure: banana has that warm, vibrant feel that screams Summer, and this drink absolutely takes full advantage of that sunshine-in-a-glass energy.

It's like a dreamy milkshake with a twist, where the banana takes center stage, but it's the subtler notes *(like the rich coffee syrup)* that really help to elevate it.

Perfect for when you're craving something indulgent but still refreshing enough for those sunny summer days.

FLAVOR PROFILES:
sweet, creamy, rich

RECIPE
SINGLE SERVING

DIRECTIONS:

- Add all ingredients EXCEPT garnish into your blender with ice.
- Blend for 90 seconds.
- Pour into your hurricane glass.
- Add your garnish on top.
- Enjoy this tropical banana concoction!

INGREDIENTS:

- 1/2 Banana
- 3 oz Banana Syrup
- 1 oz N/A Espresso Martini Mix
- 1 oz Whole Milk
- 3 oz Half and Half
- (Optional) 1 oz N/A White Rum
- 1 Cup of Ice
- Garnish: Banana slice

Today we will be making an...

ORIGINAL

mocktail

These recipes are truly my pride and joy. While a few are loosely inspired by classic cocktails, most are entirely original mocktail creations of my own. I can confidently say that crafting and writing this section was the most fun I had throughout the process of creating this book. From drinks made with cotton candy or herbal tea, to concoctions designed to capture the emotions of obsessive love and heartbreak, this section truly has it all.

SWEET BLUE HAZE
NON-ALCOHOLIC

I've wanted to make a cotton candy drink for some time as I've always thought cotton candy as a form of garnish is absolutely gorgeous.

This drink was the result of a lot of experimenting and failed attempts. It was quite difficult to balance the sweetness of a cotton candy syrup while still having the drink taste like ... well cotton candy.

However I can confidently say the end result totally achieved this. I paired the cotton candy syrup with some organic coconut for substance, lime juice for a sour effect, and just a touch of passion fruit to really brighten up the flavors in the drink.

This drink's easy, fun, and just an overall good time without being too serious.

FLAVOR PROFILES:
sweet, sour, bright

RECIPE
SINGLE SERVING

DIRECTIONS:

- Add all ingredients EXCEPT garnish and Sprite into your shaker with a handful of ice.
- Shake vigorously for 30 seconds.
- Strain into a Collins glass over ice.
- Top with your Sprite.
- Add your garnish on top.
- Take a sip of this beautiful bright blue concoction!

INGREDIENTS:

- 1.75 oz Blue Cotton Candy Syrup
- 1 oz Lime Juice
- 0.25 Passion Fruit Syrup
- 0.5 oz Organic Coconut Blend
- Sprite
- (Optional) Grapefruit Bitters
- Garnish: Blue cotton candy

YUZU GARDEN
NON-ALCOHOLIC

Yuzu ... if you haven't tried it yet, get ready for a wild ride! This citrus is a total flavor powerhouse, packed with herbal, tangy goodness that you didn't know you were missing. It's like a citrus explosion with a dash of sophistication. Now, here's the thing: Yuzu doesn't exactly show up in a ton of drinks ... yet. But I'm on a mission to change that! So, for the original version of this drink, I may or may not have taken every herbal flavor I had lying around and just tossed it in the mix ... no shame! And with some editing I was able to come up with a deliciously balanced concoction.

So, if you're the type who loves that fresh, zesty kick with a side of floral, botanical goodness, this one's for you. It's the perfect blend of complex and refreshing, with just the right amount of everything. Give it a try; you'll wonder why it took you so long to meet Yuzu!

FLAVOR PROFILES:
botanical, sweet, sour

RECIPE
SINGLE SERVING

DIRECTIONS:

- Add all ingredients EXCEPT garnish into your shaker with a handful of ice.
- Shake vigorously for 30 seconds.
- Strain into a rocks glass with ice.
- Add your garnish on top.
- Savor this herbal citrusy combination!

INGREDIENTS:

- 1.5 oz N/A Gin
- 1.5 oz Yuzu Juice
- 0.5 oz Elderflower Syrup
- 0.25 oz Rosemary Syrup (recipe page 164)
- (Optional) 2 Dashes Lemon Bitters
- Garnish: Rosemary sprig

ROCKS GLASS

GREEN MEADOW MIST
NON-ALCOHOLIC

Kiwi ... oh, how I love thee, but why aren't you gracing more drinks? Well, I decided to take this matter into my own hands and bring this fruity star into recognition with a beautifully light and botanical concoction that's truly kiwi-licious. The magic of kiwi, in my humble opinion, lies in that unforgettable aftertaste, a little tangy, a little sweet, but totally unique.

To my delight, the kiwi puree I got my hands on brought that same zing, making it the perfect match for this drink. Kiwi's natural sweetness and savory vibe needed a little counterbalance, so I brought in elderflower, rosemary, and N/A gin to create a botanical harmony.

It's like a kiwi kicked back in a botanical garden, and the results are nothing short of spectacular.

FLAVOR PROFILES:
sweet, sour, botanical

RECIPE
SINGLE SERVING

DIRECTIONS:

- Add all ingredients EXCEPT garnish and tonic soda mix into your shaker with a handful of ice.
- Shake vigorously for 30 seconds.
- Double strain into your chilled flute glass.
- Top with an equal mix of tonic and club soda.
- Add your garnish on top.
- Enjoy this beautifully botanical treat!

INGREDIENTS:

- 1.5 oz N/A Gin
- 1.5 oz Kiwi Puree
- 0.5 oz Lemon Juice
- 0.25 oz Lime Juice
- 0.5 oz Elderflower Syrup
- 0.15 oz Rosemary Syrup (recipe page 164)
- Tonic and Club Soda
- Garnish: Rosemary sprig (optional: light on fire)

MOM'S BLUEBERRY GROVE NON-ALCOHOLIC

This was one of three original drinks I created for a special event hosted by The Association of Food and Drug Officials, but its name comes from a much more personal endorsement. It quickly became one of my Mom's all-time favorite mocktails. And honestly, I get it. This drink is a complex creation that very loosely riffs on a classic gin and tonic but stands completely on its own.

It's the kind of drink that makes you pause mid-sip, trying to unravel each distinct flavor. It's a flavor puzzle in a glass with every sip turning into a new discovery.

Along with this drink comes a huge thank you to my mom for always supporting and helping me execute my ideas no matter how crazy they are *(like this book)*.

FLAVOR PROFILES:
fresh, botanical, sour

RECIPE
SINGLE SERVING

DIRECTIONS:

- Add all ingredients EXCEPT garnish and tonic into your shaker with a handful of ice.
- Shake vigorously for 30 seconds.
- Strain into your collins glass over ice.
- Top with an equal mix of tonic and club soda.
- Add your garnish on top.
- Enjoy this addictively delicious drink.

INGREDIENTS:

- 1.5 oz N/A Gin
- 4 Fresh Blueberries
- 1 oz Lemon Juice
- 1 oz Blueberry Syrup
- 0.5 oz Elderflower Syrup
- 0.15 oz Rosemary Syrup (recipe page 164)
- Tonic and Club Soda
- Garnish: Blueberries

COLLINS GLASS

COCONOAH
NON-ALCOHOLIC

This drink was made for my good friend Noah who has been featured in many of my videos. He's a big fan of raspberry and energy drinks so I came up with a unique tropical recipe that he would love.

The result is a combination of coconut and berry that is to die for. The balance of sweet, sour, and savory that this drink displays is remarkable. The addition of the can balanced on the top also adds an interactive aspect, even if it may make it a bit difficult to drink without a straw.

It also ensures a nice balance of flavors with the can dispensing more Coconut Red Bull as the drink content gets lower. If you enjoy energy drinks, coconut, or raspberry, this drink is absolutely worth a try.

FLAVOR PROFILES:
sweet, tropical, sour

RECIPE
SINGLE SERVING

DIRECTIONS:

- Add all ingredients EXCEPT garnish and Redbull into your shaker with a handful of ice.
- Shake vigorously for 30 seconds.
- Strain into your Collins glass over ice.
- Balance your Red Bull can on the top of the drink. (*Check out my video making this drink for an example.*)
- Add your garnish on top.
- Enjoy every energizing sip of this berry filled drink!

INGREDIENTS:

- 2 oz Organic Coconut Extract
- 1.5 oz Raspberry Puree
- Barspoon of Cream of Coconut
- 0.75 oz Lime Juice
- Coconut Red Bull Energy Drink
- Garnish: Raspberries

COLLINS GLASS

APRICOT DAYDREAM
NON-ALCOHOLIC

Apricots offer a uniquely sweet and tart flavor that I've always thought would go really well in a drink. This drink utilizes apricot jam and a bit of maple syrup to add a bit more sweetness. It also incorporates pear juice to really round out the more pronounced apricot notes.

The end result is perfectly refreshing and bright at the same time. The apricot is the star of the show without being too overpowering and the sweetness is subtle enough to enhance the drink without overwhelming it. The fresh mint sprig also adds some nice aromatic elements that really help pronounce the fresh flavors in this drink.

If you're a fan of apricots or sweet summery *(yes, I know that's not a word)* drinks this is the perfect choice for you.

FLAVOR PROFILES:
fresh, herbal, sweet

RECIPE
SINGLE SERVING

DIRECTIONS:

- Add all ingredients EXCEPT garnish and club soda into your shaker with a handful of ice.
- Shake vigorously for 30 seconds.
- Strain into your rocks glass over ice.
- Top with club soda.
- Add your garnish on top.
- You'll be daydreaming about this drink for weeks!

INGREDIENTS:

- 1 oz Apricot Jam
- 0.75 Lemon Juice
- 0.5 oz Maple Syrup
- 1.5 oz Pear Juice
- Club Soda
- (Optional) 2 Dashes Cardamom Bitters
- Garnish: Apricot and mint sprig

ROCKS GLASS

FIZZ DE VIOLETTE
NON-ALCOHOLIC

A non-alcoholic Ramos Gin Fizz was one of the drinks featured in my first book and is still one of my favorite non-alcoholic variations on a classic cocktail to this day. This is loosely based on that drink, but brings it to a whole other level.

Lavender can be used as a very effective aromatic and is in turn a perfect addition to the foam in this drink leading to the drink both tasting and smelling delicious.

It also utilizes crushed up lavender buds (edible) on top for garnish to really complete the breathtaking aesthetic of this mocktail.

It's no easy task getting the foam to properly rise up out of the glass, but if you can pull it off, it's totally worth it.

FLAVOR PROFILES:
sweet, botanical, sour

RECIPE
SINGLE SERVING

DIRECTIONS:

- Add all ingredients EXCEPT garnish and tonic into your shaker.
- Dry shake first for 45 seconds.
- Shake vigorously with 3 medium ice cubes until they dissolve.
- Strain into your chilled Collins glass and let sit refrigerated for 90 seconds.
- Create a small hole in the foam in the middle and gently pour the chilled tonic in until the foam rises past the top of the glass.
- Pour your crushed up lavender buds gently on the foam.
- High five! You did it! Enjoy your delicious drink!

INGREDIENTS:

- 1.5 oz N/A Gin
- 1 oz Lavender Syrup
- 1 oz Heavy Cream
- 1 Egg White
- 1 oz Lemon Juice
- 0.5 oz Honey Syrup (recipe page 165)
- Elderflower Tonic
- Garnish: Lavender buds

SIPPIN SAGE
NON-ALCOHOLIC

Full transparency, I came up with the name for this drink before actually coming up with the recipe. I knew I wanted it to be herbal and light while still being full of sage's distinct earthy and savory flavor. I ended up settling on a green apple extract for the fruit base that wasn't too sweet but would go well with the earthy notes in the sage. I added honey syrup for sweetness, however, considering the drink is shaken, a slightly smaller portion of honey will also do the trick. The result at this point was overly sweet and the sage wasn't showing up as much as I wanted. After some experimenting I added 2 oz of tonic to the drink after shaking. It perfectly balanced the sweetness and added some nice bitter flavors.

In the end, this drink was a labor of love that exceeded my already high expectations.

FLAVOR PROFILES:
earthy, sweet, dry

RECIPE
SINGLE SERVING

DIRECTIONS:

- Muddle sage in the bottom of the shaker.
- Add all ingredients EXCEPT garnish and tonic into your shaker with a handful of ice.
- Shake vigorously for 30 seconds.
- Double strain into your rocks glass over ice.
- Top with tonic.
- Add your garnish on top.
- Enjoy this savory sage filled delight!

INGREDIENTS:

- 6-8 Sage Leaves
- 2.5 oz Green Apple Extract (recipe page 162)
- 1 oz Honey Syrup
- 0.5 oz Lemon Juice
- Elderflower Tonic (Regular will work too.)
- Garnish: Green apples and sage leaves

ROCKS GLASS

VELVET LEX
NON-ALCOHOLIC

I designed this drink for my friend Alexis, one of my coworkers from my first bartending job and a good friend of mine. She loves blackberry and citrus but isn't a big fan of carbonation and overly sweet drinks.

In the end I decided to do a more modernized variation of a classic bramble that results in a pleasantly sweet, herbal, and tart drink that's absolutely delicious.

I also used egg white to produce a beautiful foam on top to really pull together the already breathtaking presentation of this drink.

If you're a fan of blackberry or the Blackberry Bramble from my first book, you should definitely give this one a try.

FLAVOR PROFILES:
botanical, rich, sour

RECIPE
SINGLE SERVING

DIRECTIONS:

- Muddle blackberries in the bottom of the shaker.
- Add all ingredients EXCEPT garnish into your shaker with a handful of ice.
- Shake vigorously for 30 seconds.
- Strain into your rocks glass over ice.
- Add your garnish on top.
- Savor this purple beauty!

INGREDIENTS:

- 1.5 oz N/A Gin
- 4-6 Fresh Blackberries
- 1 oz Blackberry Syrup
- 0.5 oz Pear Puree
- 0.75 oz Lemon Juice
- (optional) 2 Dashes Lemon Bitters
- 1 Egg White
- Garnish: Blackberries

ROCKS GLASS

LIQUID LIMERENCE
NON-ALCOHOLIC

I always make drinks centered around ingredients or flavors but never emotions. This drink's description reads more as a poem than a drink description, but it's truly beautiful.

A drink that captures the electric high of infatuation and the quiet ache it leaves behind. It opens with a sharp kiss of tamarind. It's tart, bold, impossible to ignore, softened by delicate coconut water, and a whisper of sweet orgeat, like the sweetness you imagine between glances. Pineapple juice adds bright and exciting flavors, mimicking that rush in your chest when they look your way. But beneath the surface, there's depth; a touch of angostura and sour lime to echo the tart bitter longing, the overthinking, the waiting. It's beautiful, intoxicating … and just a little bittersweet. Like falling for someone, who hasn't fallen back.

FLAVOR PROFILES:
bittersweet, tangy, sour

RECIPE
SINGLE SERVING

DIRECTIONS:

- Add all ingredients EXCEPT garnish into your shaker with a handful of ice.
- Shake vigorously for 30 seconds.
- Double strain into your chilled coupe glass.
- Add your garnish on the glass.
- Feel the terrifying infatuation in every sip.

INGREDIENTS:

- 1 oz Tamarind Syrup
- 0.5 oz Orgeat
- 0.75 oz Lime Juice
- 2 oz Pineapple Juice
- 1 oz Coconut Water
- 1 Dash Aromatic Bitters
- Garnish: Heart shaped orange peel

BLACK-BERRY-CHERRY SPRITZ
NON-ALCOHOLIC

The space between "black" and "berry" isn't a typo ... it's intentional! This drink blends both blackberry and black cherry to create a seriously savory rich combo. It was inspired by one of my all-time favorite recipes from my first book, the Blackberry Bramble. If you've seen the original, you'll notice the familiar presentation. There are definitely some twists in this version, but the roots are still there.

Does it beat the classic? Hard to say, but the addition of black cherry brings some exciting new flavors that, according to some who've tasted it, might just be a favorite over the original.

Either way, it's a fresh spin that's sure to leave your taste buds satisfied!

FLAVOR PROFILES:
sour, sweet, rich

RECIPE
SINGLE SERVING

DIRECTIONS:

- Add all ingredients EXCEPT garnish and Stella Rosa into your shaker with a handful of ice.
- Shake vigorously for 30 seconds.
- Strain into your rocks glass over ice.
- Top with Stella Rosa Black.
- Add your garnish on top.
- Enjoy every sip of this berry filled treat!

INGREDIENTS:

- 1.5 oz N/A Gin
- 0.75 oz Black Cherry Syrup
- 1 oz Blackberry Syrup
- 1 oz Lemon Juice
- N/A Stella Rosa Black
- Garnish: Lemon twist with a blackberry and Luxardo cherry.

ROCKS GLASS

AUTUMN GINGER
NON-ALCOHOLIC

This drink was actually created for my ex-girlfriend. That intro may throw some people, *(and rightfully so)* but we've been on good terms as friends for years and I always promised I'd devote a drink to her in one of my books. She's a huge fan of ginger and apples so this drink incorporates both.

It also uses a Lapsang Souchong smoky Black Tea. This adds some unique depth and smoky flavors.

The drink is designed to emulate Fall scents and flavors such as apples and burning leaf piles. She also has red hair, so I had to sneak ginger into the name somehow.

If you want to drink autumn in a glass with some hints of ginger, this is the perfect drink for you.

FLAVOR PROFILES:
smokey, herbal, sweet

RECIPE
SINGLE SERVING

DIRECTIONS:

- Add all ingredients EXCEPT garnish into your shaker with a handful of ice.
- Shake vigorously for 30 seconds.
- Strain into your rocks glass over ice.
- Add your garnish on top and light it on fire.
- Savor this toasty Autumn drink!

INGREDIENTS:

- 2.5 oz Lapsang Souchong Black Tea
- 1.25 oz Apple Syrup
- 0.5 oz Ginger Syrup
- 0.75 oz Lemon Juice
- 2 Dashes Aromatic Bitters
- Garnish: Fresh thyme lit on fire.

ROCKS GLASS

AGAVE PUNCH NO. 3
NON-ALCOHOLIC

I almost put this drink into the "inspired" category but considering it's a variation on the Agave Punch No.2 from my previous book, which is of course a variation on the original Agave Punch. I figured it's safe to say it's a fairly original recipe. This recipe plays around with acid adjustment, which is the process of adding Malic or Citric acid to create an added acidity to mimic citruses, such as lemon and lime. I know all that sounds a bit complicated, but it's actually not too bad, and is relatively inexpensive.

It also creates an astoundingly distinct flavor with the orange still tasting like orange, but with the acidity of something closer to pineapple.

This drink is a great intro to the world of micro mixology and an overall wonderfully balanced drink.

FLAVOR PROFILES:
sour, sweet, citrusy

RECIPE
SINGLE SERVING

DIRECTIONS:

- Add all ingredients EXCEPT garnish into your shaker with a handful of ice.
- Shake vigorously for 30 seconds.
- Double Strain into your chilled coupe glass.
- Add your garnish on the glass.
- Enjoy this deceptively sour and citrusy drink!

INGREDIENTS:

- 4 oz Orange Juice
- 1 oz Agave Syrup
- 0.75 g Malic Acid
- 3 Dashes Orange Bitters
- Garnish: Orange zest

POM BERRY FIZZ
NON-ALCOHOLIC

I originally created this drink for a special event at my job as a bartender at a craft cocktail bar. It was such a hit that I knew it had to be included in my book. The response was overwhelmingly positive … not just from guests, but from colleagues as well, and it even ended up being featured during an interview on WGN.

What makes this mocktail stand out is how each individual ingredient brings something essential to the overall experience. Every flavor plays a distinct role, yet they come together in perfect harmony.

It's a refreshing, balanced drink that I believe anyone *(regardless of age or preference)* can truly enjoy. The flavors are familiar, yet elevated, making it a universally appealing option for any occasion.

FLAVOR PROFILES:
sour, savory, bubbly

RECIPE
SINGLE SERVING

DIRECTIONS:

- Add all ingredients EXCEPT garnish and San Pellegrino into your shaker with a handful of ice.
- Shake vigorously for 30 seconds.
- Strain into your collins glass over ice.
- Top with your San Pellegrino.
- Add your garnish on top.
- Enjoy the pomegranate perfection!

INGREDIENTS:

- 2 oz Strawberry Puree
- 0.75 oz Ube
- 1 oz Lemon Juice
- 2 Dashes Plum Bitters
- San Pellegrino Pomegranate & Orange
- Garnish: Strawberry

COLLINS GLASS

FRIE IN THE DARK
NON-ALCOHOLIC

There are plenty of sweet sugary coffee drinks out there *(and in this book)*, but with this drink I wanted to try something different.

My goal was to create a balanced spicy coffee drink without overwhelming the flavor of well ... coffee. In the end it took quite a few tries, and at least a couple glasses of milk to cleanse my palate, but the end result was totally worth it.

The spice ends up elevating the coffee notes and the subtle notes of cacao from the chocolate bitters helps really round out all the different flavors while not overpowering any of them.

While the spice or coffee in this drink might turn some people away, for those that remain this drink is totally worth a try.

FLAVOR PROFILES:
spicy, rich, sweet

RECIPE
SINGLE SERVING

DIRECTIONS:

- Add all ingredients EXCEPT garnish into your shaker with a handful of ice.
- Shake vigorously for 30 seconds.
- Double strain into your chilled coupe glass.
- Shave chocolate over the top and add your garnish.
- Savor this spicy caffeinated concoction!

INGREDIENTS:

- 3 oz Unsweetened Cold Brew Coffee
- 0.5 oz Habanero Syrup (recipe page 166)
- 0.5 oz Demerara Syrup (recipe page 161)
- 3 Dashes Aztec Chocolate Bitters
- Milk Chocolate
- Garnish: Habanero pepper slice.

COUPE GLASS

PEACH MEADOW
NON-ALCOHOLIC

While herbal, botanical, and peach may not sound like the best combo it's shockingly good. This drink employs the botanicals from a non-alcoholic gin and the widely unknown herbal qualities of some freshly muddled raspberries and balances them perfectly with peaches' brighter vibrantly sweet essence.

While this drink still has a nice sweetness to it, it's also somewhat bitter and herbaceous, creating a truly unique result.

Instead of the flavors clashing, they complement each other and create a tasting experience that will have you returning for another sip over and over.

So, enjoy this deliciously herbal peach treat!

FLAVOR PROFILES:
sweet, herbal, sour

RECIPE
SINGLE SERVING

DIRECTIONS:

- Muddle 3 fresh raspberries in a mixing glass.
- Add all ingredients EXCEPT garnish and tonic into your mixing glass with a handful of ice.
- Stir for 30 seconds.
- Double Strain into your chilled flute glass.
- Top with your tonic.
- Add your garnish on the glass.
- Enjoy this herbal peachy mix!

INGREDIENTS:

- 3 fresh Raspberries
- 1.5 oz Peach Puree
- 1.5 oz N/A Gin
- 0.5 oz Honey Syrup (recipe page 165)
- 0.5 oz Lemon Juice
- Tonic
- Garnish: Peach chunk and mint sprig.

FLUTE GLASS

LYCHEE WHISPER
NON-ALCOHOLIC

Lychee is a truly unique fruit. It has very bright and floral flavors that most remind me of a grape, but at the same time are very different. While Lychee by itself is by no means my favorite flavor in drinks; I wanted to challenge myself to make something delicious with it. I absolutely succeeded! This drink is a perfect mix of sweet, tart, floral, and bitter.

The goal of any good drink is to enhance a key ingredient or flavor ... in this case Lychee. This mocktail absolutely achieves that, creating a drink that's perfect to sip on and enjoy without any of its flavors being too overpowering.

Whether you're a diehard fan of Lychee, or trying it for the first time, this drink is a wonderful choice.

FLAVOR PROFILES:
botanical, bubbly, sweet

RECIPE
SINGLE SERVING

DIRECTIONS:

- Add all ingredients EXCEPT garnish and tonic into your mixing glass with a handful of ice.
- Stir for 30 seconds.
- Strain into your chilled coupe glass.
- Top with your elderflower tonic.
- Add your garnish on top.
- Notice the gentle whisper of the sweet and tart flavors!

INGREDIENTS:

- 1.5 oz Lychee Syrup
- 0.5 oz Yuzu Juice
- 0.75 oz Grapefruit Juice
- 1.5 oz Chilled Jasmine Tea
- Elderflower Tonic
- Garnish: Grapefruit slice

COCO BLOOM
NON-ALCOHOLIC

Coconut and cucumber might not be the most obvious pairing, but together they create an incredibly refreshing and delicious balance.

The cucumber brings a crisp, clean, almost cooling quality … it's light, vegetal, and thirst-quenching. Meanwhile, the coconut adds a soft, creamy richness with a subtle almost fruity sweetness that rounds everything out. With the other added herbal and sour notes this balances out into one of the more unique but perfectly balanced mocktails in this book.

I'm not sure if anyone else has tried the combo of coconut and cucumber, but there definitely needs to be more done with it.

Again, this is really just one of those drinks that sounds crazy, and maybe even gross, until you try it.

FLAVOR PROFILES:
herbal, tropical, sour

RECIPE
SINGLE SERVING

DIRECTIONS:

- Add all ingredients EXCEPT garnish and club soda into your shaker with a handful of ice.
- Shake vigorously for 30 seconds.
- Strain into your Collins glass over ice.
- Top with your club soda.
- Add your garnish on top.
- Enjoy this refreshing coconut extravaganza. Cheers!

INGREDIENTS:

- 1.5 oz Organic Coconut Blend
- 0.5 oz Elderflower Syrup
- 0.5 oz Lime Juice
- 0.5 oz Cucumber Extract (recipe page 167)
- 1 oz Chilled Jasmine Tea
- Club Soda
- Garnish: Lime wheel and dried coconut

COLLINS GLASS

CARMINE COPPICE
NON-ALCOHOLIC

Cranberry is often utilized as a tarter component in drinks, but its unrecognized sweet element can also be quite delicious. This drink makes use of that with a cranberry syrup that still captures cranberries tart notes along with its sweeter ones.

It also adds some nice complementary herbal notes in the form of elderflower syrup, rosemary syrup, and green tea. Finally, it's topped with Canada Dry Ginger Cranberry Soda. It's a delicious combination that's so different from most other cranberry centered concoctions.

As for the name: carmine means a vivid crimson color and coppice is an area of woodland with thick bushes. This is a reference to the drinks color and subtle herbal notes.

FLAVOR PROFILES:
tart, sour, sweet

RECIPE
SINGLE SERVING

DIRECTIONS:

- Add all ingredients EXCEPT garnish and Canada Dry into your shaker with a handful of ice.
- Shake vigorously for 30 seconds.
- Double strain into your chilled coupe glass.
- Top with your Canada Dry Ginger Cranberry Soda.
- Add your garnish on top.
- Relish this red refreshment!

INGREDIENTS:

- 1 oz Cranberry Syrup
- 0.5 oz Elderflower Syrup
- 0.25 oz Rosemary Syrup (recipe page 164)
- 0.75 oz Lime Juice
- 2 oz Chilled Jasmine Tea
- Canada Dry Ginger Cranberry Soda
- Garnish: Cranberries and Rosemary

ANISE REVERIE
NON-ALCOHOLIC

This drink, as the name suggests, is based around the unique flavor that is Anise.

I used Sobreo's Vietnamese Star Anise to achieve a distinct anise flavor without overpowering the drink.

Anise is often used as a cooking spice, so it has a tendency to overpower most drinks it's in.

I avoided this by adding a bit of tamarind syrup which is very tart and sweet and helps offset the anise's stronger notes.

The end result is a pleasantly sweet and tart drink that showcases some truly unique favors that will have you going back for a second sip to identify them all.

FLAVOR PROFILES:
sweet, aromatic, tangy

RECIPE
SINGLE SERVING

DIRECTIONS:

- Add all ingredients EXCEPT garnish into your shaker with a handful of ice.
- Shake vigorously for 30 seconds.
- Double strain into your chilled coupe glass.
- Add your garnish on top.
- Sip on this amazingly aromatic concoction!

INGREDIENTS:

- 2.5 oz Sobrco Vietnamese Star Anise
- 1 oz Lime Juice
- 0.75 oz Ginger Syrup
- 0.5 oz Tamarind Syrup
- 2 Dashes Aromatic Bitters
- (optional) Egg White for foam
- Garnish: Anise Pod

DESERT SILK
NON-ALCOHOLIC

Prickly pear and hibiscus is a combo of flavors I've been wanting to try something with for a while, and this drink is the culmination of that desire. Prickly pear offers a sweeter and savory flavor, with the hibiscus tea bringing in a sharper tart component that pairs beautifully.

The honey and ginger syrup also add a bit more depth that really increases the complexity of the drink. Finally, while the rhubarb bitters are optional, they do really add a nice layer of tartness to the drink that elevates the hibiscus to a whole new level.

A lot of the flavors in this drink sound overpowering and very niche. I can assure the final product really does appeal to a wide audience, is generally well balanced, and is an enjoyable drink with a beautiful color.

FLAVOR PROFILES:
sweet, sour, herbal

RECIPE
SINGLE SERVING

DIRECTIONS:

- Add all ingredients EXCEPT garnish into your shaker with a handful of ice.
- Shake vigorously for 30 seconds.
- Double strain into your chilled coupe glass.
- Add your garnish on top.
- Enjoy this crazy culmination of flavors!

INGREDIENTS:

- 1.5 oz Prickly Pear Puree
- 2 oz Strong Hibiscus Tea
- 0.75 oz Lemon Juice
- 0.5 oz Ginger Syrup
- 0.5 oz Honey Syrup (recipe page 165)
- (Optional) 2 Dashes Rhubarb Bitters
- Garnish: Lemon twist and hibiscus flower

MICHIGAN BLAZING ORCHARD NON-ALCOHOLIC

This was again one of the three drinks I designed around an event for The Association of Food and Drug Officials. This drink is based on my home state of Michigan's reputation for growing delicious apples.

Now admittedly, I'm not a huge fan of apples in drinks, but even I can admit this one is absolutely tasty.

It's got a nice bit of kick that really elevates the apple and leads to an amazingly balanced drink that reaches a wide appeal.

I never would have expected spicy flavors and apple to work this well together but WOW!

Finally, the sparkling apple on top really completes the drink and cuts a bit of the spiciness.

FLAVOR PROFILES:
spicy, bubbly, sweet

RECIPE
SINGLE SERVING

DIRECTIONS:

- Add all ingredients EXCEPT garnish into your shaker with a handful of ice.
- Shake vigorously for 30 seconds.
- Double strain into your chilled flute glass.
- Add your garnish on top.
- Enjoy this spicy apple mixture!

INGREDIENTS:

- 1.5 oz N/A Tequila (Ritual for spiciness)
- 1 oz Apple Syrup
- 0.75 oz Lemon Juice
- 0.5 oz Ginger Syrup
- Sparkling Apple (Martinelli's)
- Garnish: Apple peel

PEACH PLEASE
NON-ALCOHOLIC

This drink originated from me challenging myself to make a drink with one of my favorite fruits (peach) using other flavors that have never been mixed with peach before. The result was a truly unique drink that balances out surprisingly well. Grapefruit and peach is an interesting combo that works together surprisingly well.

The sweetness from the agave helps balance out the other flavors while still contributing to the slightly bitter aftertaste.

Finally, I once again made use of a Lapsang Souchong smoky black tea to really add depth to this drink.

If you enjoy peaches and want to try something new and unique, this drink is the perfect choice.

FLAVOR PROFILES:
sweet, fresh, sour

RECIPE
SINGLE SERVING

DIRECTIONS:

- Add all ingredients EXCEPT garnish into your shaker with a handful of ice.
- Shake vigorously for 30 seconds.
- Strain into your rocks glass over ice.
- Add your garnish on top.
- Take a sip of this unique peachy creation!

INGREDIENTS:

- 1.5 oz Peach Puree
- 1 oz Grapefruit Juice
- 0.5 oz Agave Syrup
- 2 oz Lapsang Souchong Black Tea
- (optional) 2 Dashes Peach Bitters
- Garnish: Rolled flower made out of peach skin.

ROCKS GLASS

CRIMSON CASCADE
NON-ALCOHOLIC

I'll be honest, I've never been a big fan of non-alcoholic aperitifs. They tend to be bitter, dry, and just don't sit right with my palate. But instead of writing them off completely, I decided to challenge myself: could I create a drink where a non-alcoholic aperitif was still the star … that I actually enjoyed?

After a whole lot of trial and error *(and maybe a few borderline disasters)*, I finally cracked the code. This drink hits that sweet spot *(literally and figuratively)*. The strawberry and non-alcoholic Moscato bring in a bright, juicy sweetness, while the yuzu and peach bitters add depth and complexity that rounds everything out.

Together, they transform the aperitif from something I'd normally avoid, into something I can't stop sipping.

FLAVOR PROFILES:
sweet, bitter, sour

RECIPE
SINGLE SERVING

DIRECTIONS:

- Add all ingredients EXCEPT garnish into your shaker with a handful of ice.
- Shake vigorously for 30 seconds.
- Double strain into your chilled flute glass.
- Top with your club soda.
- Add your garnish on top.
- Take a sip of this crafty crimson creation!

INGREDIENTS:

- 1 oz N/A Aperitif
- 2 oz N/A Moscato (Not sparkling)
- 1 oz Yuzu Juice
- 0.5 oz Strawberry Puree
- 2 Dashes Peach Bitters
- Club Soda
- Garnish: Strawberry slice

THE LAST SIP
NON-ALCOHOLIC

This drink has quite the story behind it. My bar manager Teo made me a bet revolving around me getting all the drink orders out within 15 minutes or less, no matter how large the order.

His condition, if I failed, was that he'd get to add a drink into my book. Spoiler ... he won. One order was only over the 15-minute mark by 20 seconds ... voila this drink was born.

It's a refreshing and slightly spicy mocktail that appeals to pretty much anyone. It's sweet, sour, botanical, and has a small touch of spice that really helps bring the drink together.

And as for the name, Teo gave me the recipe a week before this book needed to be finished, so it's the last recipe in the book, hence it being named "The Last Sip".

FLAVOR PROFILES:
spicy, sweet, bubbly

RECIPE
SINGLE SERVING

DIRECTIONS:

- Add all ingredients EXCEPT garnish and Tost into your shaker with a handful of ice.
- Shake vigorously for 30 seconds.
- Strain into your Collins glass over ice.
- Top with Tost Sparkling White Tea.
- Add your garnish on top.
- Enjoy the sweet spicy kick!

INGREDIENTS:

- 1.5 oz N/A Tequila
- 0.75 oz Yuzu Juice
- Bar Spoon Jalapeno Extract
- 0.5 oz Peach Syrup
- 0.75 oz Lemon Juice
- 0.25 oz Rosemary Syrup (recipe page 164)
- Tost Sparkling White Tea
- Garnish: Orange peal

COLLINS GLASS

mocktail · INGREDIENT RECIPES

What follows are instructions for how to make some of the ingredients featured in the recipes throughout this book. These are some ingredients that I personally think are most beneficial to make yourself to either save money or just create a higher quality ingredient. While you are able to buy most of these pre-made; it adds an extra level of satisfaction knowing you made it yourself.

DEMERARA SYRUP RECIPE

DIRECTIONS:

- Heat the water in the saucepan until it's warm (not boiling).
- Add sugars and stir until they're fully dissolved.
- Let cool for about 20 minutes.
- Transfer to a bottle using a funnel, wait to cap until it's luke warm.

INGREDIENTS:

- 1 ¼ cups Demerara Sugar
- ½ cup Plain Sugar
- 1 cup Water

TOOLS NEEDED:

- Saucepan
- Stove
- Bottle
- Funnel
- Ladle

GREEN APPLE EXTRACT RECIPE

DIRECTIONS:

- Add all ingredients into your blender and blend for roughly one minute.
- Pour into a fine strainer with cheesecloth over a bowl.
- Wait for the extract to strain then transfer with a funnel to a bottle.

INGREDIENTS:

- 1 Whole Green Apple
- ⅙ cup Sugar
- ⅓ cup Water
- 1.5 tsp Malic Acid

TOOLS NEEDED:

- Blender or something similar
- Fine Strainer
- Cheesecloth
- Funnel
- Bottle

20% SALINE SOLUTION RECIPE

DIRECTIONS:

- Add all ingredients into a mixing glass (you can adjust the amount based on bottle size).
- Stir until the salt is completely dissolved.
- Pour into a bottle that you can attach a dropper to using a funnel.

INGREDIENTS:

- 2 oz Salt (the higher the quality the better)
- 8 oz very hot but not boiling water

TOOLS NEEDED:

- Mixing glass or large glass
- Funnel
- Bar spoon to stir
- Bottle

ROSEMARY SYRUP RECIPE

DIRECTIONS:

- Combine sugar and water in a saucepan and heat until the sugar dissolves and starts to simmer.
- Turn off the heat and add the rosemary chopped into smaller pieces (for better aromatic effect).
- Cover the pan with a lid or plate and steep for 30 minutes.
- Pour over a strainer into a bowl and allow to cool before transferring to a glass bottle and capping.

INGREDIENTS:

- Roughly 25 g Rosemary (8-10 large sprigs)
- ½ cup Sugar
- ½ cup Water

TOOLS NEEDED:

- Saucepan (preferably with a lid)
- Strainer
- Stove
- Bowl
- Bottle
- Funnel

HONEY SYRUP RECIPE

DIRECTIONS:

- Heat the water in the saucepan until it's warm (not boiling)
- Add honey and stir until fully dissolved.
- Let cool for about 10-15 minutes.
- Transfer to a bottle using a funnel, wait to cap until its luke warm.

INGREDIENTS:

- 1 ⅓ cups Honey
- 1 ½ cups Water

TOOLS NEEDED:

- Saucepan
- Stove
- Bottle
- Funnel
- Ladle

HABANERO SYRUP RECIPE

DIRECTIONS:

- Combine sugar and water in a saucepan over medium heat and stir until the sugar dissolves.
- Add sliced up habaneros into the pan and let simmer for 5-10 minutes (taste as you go to determine preference).
- Turn off the heat and allow to steep for 15 - 20 minutes.
- Strain into your bottle using a funnel and allow to cool to luke warm temperature before capping.

INGREDIENTS:

- 2 Habanero Peppers (add seeds for extra spice)
- 1 ½ cups Sugar
- 1 ¾ cups Water

TOOLS NEEDED:

- Saucepan
- Stove
- Bottle
- Funnel
- Ladle
- Strainer

CUCUMBER EXTRACT RECIPE

DIRECTIONS:

- Add all ingredients into your blender and blend for roughly a minute.
- Pour into a fine strainer with cheesecloth over a bowl.
- Wait until the extract strains through the cheesecloth.
- Transfer the strained liquid to a bottle with a funnel.

INGREDIENTS:

- 400 g Cucumber (1 large or 1 ½ medium cucumbers)
- 1 ¾ cups Water
- ⅓ cup Sugar
- 1 Tbsp Lemon Juice

TOOLS NEEDED:

- Blender or something similar
- Fine Strainer
- Cheesecloth
- Funnel
- Bottle

CARAMEL BUTTERSCOTCH CREAM RECIPE

DIRECTIONS:

- Add all ingredients into your mixing glass.
- For best results, stir using a handheld drink mixer.
- Taste as you go and tweak ratios to your liking.
- You can now either add the cream to a small bottle or to the top of your drink.

INGREDIENTS:

- 0.75 oz Butterscotch Ice Cream Topping
- 1 oz Salted Caramel Ice Cream Topping
- 2.5 oz Heavy Cream

TOOLS NEEDED:

- Handheld Drink Mixer
- Mixing Glass

tales of the TEENAGE BARTENDER

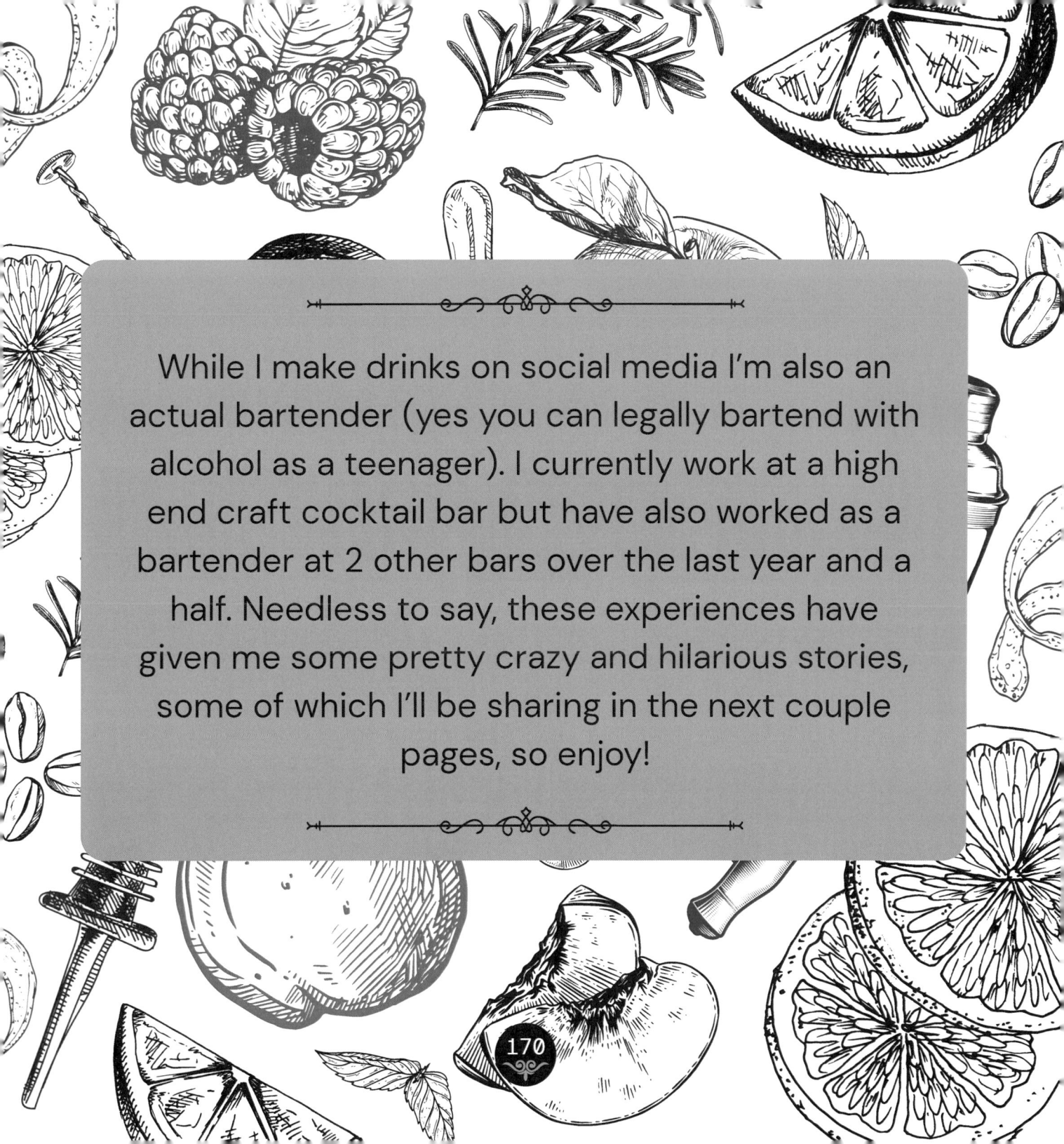

While I make drinks on social media I'm also an actual bartender (yes you can legally bartend with alcohol as a teenager). I currently work at a high end craft cocktail bar but have also worked as a bartender at 2 other bars over the last year and a half. Needless to say, these experiences have given me some pretty crazy and hilarious stories, some of which I'll be sharing in the next couple pages, so enjoy!

$5 for a Hug

It was a painfully slow Friday night … the kind where the clock seems to be actively mocking you with every tick. I was the lone bartender on duty, and not a single soul had wandered in for what felt like hours. I had already wiped down the bar three times, organized the liquor bottles out of sheer boredom, and was one Spotify ad away from losing my mind. Just as I was about to call it quits and close up shop, the door creaked open and in walked two girls.

They were clearly already a few drinks deep, and announced they were bar hopping their way around town. They ordered a couple shots, we chatted about random nonsense and then, just as quickly as they arrived, they were getting ready to leave.
That's when one of them looked at me with the confidence only tequila can provide and said, "Can I have a hug?"
Now, I was tired. My brain was already halfway back in my dorm curled up under my covers. So I politely declined. But then she upped the ante.

"I'll give you five bucks."

I'd love to say I held strong, that I'm a man of principle and integrity. But folks… five bucks is five bucks. And one slightly awkward hug later, I was five dollars richer. Then her friend, not to be outdone, pulled the same move. Suddenly I was up ten dollars and one hell of a story. They vanished into the night, giggling amidst the dim city lights, and I never saw them again.

Still one of the more random, but oddly heartwarming nights I've had behind the bar.

Unique Palette

I once had a man attempt what may still be the weirdest drink order I've ever heard. He kicked things off by confidently asking for a double shot of Everclear ... yes the 190 proof rocket fuel. I explained we didn't carry that (since I worked at a cocktail bar, not a gas station with a liquor license).

Unfazed, he scoffed and said, "No self-respecting bar would be without Everclear" and immediately pivoted to asking for Malort. I beg you to pause, go watch someone try it for the first time, and you'll understand why I started questioning reality.

I told him, nope we ran out last night, still hoping this was all some elaborate joke ... it was not.

He grew visibly irritated and then hit me with his final request. "Do you have any gluten-free vodkas?" And that folks, was the moment I truly broke. Because here's the kicker ... all unflavored vodka is gluten free. I told him this politely, while trying to keep a straight face, and asked if he had a brand in mind.

He finally landed on Ketel One ... mixed with water.

To this day I still don't know if he was trolling me, doing some weird taste-test experiment, or it I'd just met the man with the most chaotic palate in existence.

Juice Cannon

This one's not about bartending ... well, not technically. It was actually a first date. I'd been chatting with this girl for a bit and finally invited her over to watch a horror movie and make her a mocktail.

Now, keep in mind, this was early in my bartending journey ... like, "still learning what not to shake near other humans" early. I decided to make her a non-alcoholic Cherry Sour, went to shake it up and immediately realized I'd mixed up my shakers. They didn't seal properly.

If you've never shaken a drink before, here's the fun part: the liquid slams back and forth inside the shaker, building up pressure, and if it's not sealed? It's basically a pressurized juice cannon.

She was standing directly across from me. There was a 50/50 chance this exploded in my face, or hers.

I'll let you guess who caught the cherry blast. Spoiler ... it wasn't me.

She was wearing mostly white clothing and was covered (literally) head to toe in bright red liquid.

Let's just say, I never heard from her again. If she somehow ends up reading this ... I am so very sorry, but it made for what's now a pretty funny story.

Oh Snap!

This isn't one specific story, it's more of a collection of moments that all lead to the same universal truth: do not snap at your bartender. Especially, ESPECIALLY if you don't even know what drink you want to order.

You'd be amazed how many people hit me with the ol' finger snap like I'm a dog that wandered off, just to follow it up with, "Uhhhh ... what do I feel like ordering?" and then stare at the menu like they've never seen a list of drinks in their life.

It's always the same: high urgency, zero preparation.

Look, I get it... it can be hard to decide, menus can be intimidating. But, if you're not ready to order, maybe hold off on summoning me like you're desperately trying to hail a cab on a rainy night. A wave, a polite "Hey, when you get a sec.", literally *anything else* is fine.

The snap? The snap goes straight to our souls. It doesn't speed things up ... it just adds one more straw to the camel's already overworked back.

So please, for the love of all bitters and sanity, don't snap. We're doing our best out here. And that last shred of patience? Yeah... it's hanging on by a cocktail garnish.

OK ... short rant over. Cheers!

High Standards

I've had my share of eccentric managers as a bartender, but one will forever live in my memory, and not in a good way. This person had a reputation for being obsessed with cleanliness. Like, sure, a clean bar is important. But this was next-level. Think: obsessive, ritualistic, borderline spiritual devotion to sanitation.

When I first got hired, coworkers warned me. I figured they were exaggerating, maybe embellishing for laughs. "They once wiped down the ice." "They made someone re-mop because it didn't smell clean." You know your usual bartender lore. I didn't believe a word … that was until my first solo closing shift.

I went all out. Everything was spotless. Floors, bottles, sinks … hell, I even cleaned parts of the ceiling. Confident in my work, I showed up the next morning for the "cleanliness inspection".

The manager walked in for my inspection, didn't say a word, got down on their hands and knees (in their fancy clothes) … and sniffed the floor.

I stood there frozen, watching a grown adult smell tile like it held the secrets of the universe.

The verdict? "Not bad, but the floor didn't smell enough like bleach".

To this day, I've never met another manager who literally inhaled the floors. But credit where it's due; I now close a bar so well you could perform surgery on the garnish station. Unhinged? Yes. Effective? Unfortunately, also yes.

Side Hussle

I'm probably one of the youngest bartenders I know. Seriously, you don't see many 18 or even 19-year-old bartenders out in the wild… especially not slinging drinks behind a busy bar on a Friday night. Most of the time, I'm working next to people in their mid-to-late twenties, sometimes older. So naturally, when customers see me confidently mixing cocktails, pulling perfect pints, and chatting like I've been doing this for years, they just assume I'm in my early twenties.

I decided to turn that little age mystery into a bit of a fun game. Here's how it works: if you can guess my age in three tries, your next round is on me. But if you can't? You owe me three bucks. It's simple, lighthearted, and surprisingly profitable.

People get super into it, throwing out wild guesses, trying to read my face like I'm bluffing in a high-stakes poker game. I've been running this little side hustle for a while now and I'm currently up $72 and counting. Turns out adults are terrible at guessing how old someone is when that someone can whip up a margarita faster than you can Google what's in it.

Not a single person has nailed it in three tries yet. And honestly, watching people flounder on their last guess is half the fun. So yeah, I may be young, but I've got a good poker face, a solid pour, and a growing tab of other people's bad guesses.

Who says youth is wasted on the young?

STRANGE DRINK ORDERS I have received

"Let's get the Marlort combinations out of the way. If you aren't familiar with Malort, look up some videos of people trying it... you will be quite entertained!"

Malort Martini – *"Shaken or stirred? ... it probably won't make a difference."*
Malort Old-Fashioned – *"No amount of bitters can save this one."*
Malort Sour – *"Bitter and sour ... what a combo."*
Malort and Coke – *"To each their own."*
Malort Espresso Martini – *"Coffee and wormwood ... that's unique."*

Rumple Mintz Sour – *"Sour mouthwash?!?!"*

Tito's and Vodka – *"Can I see your ID again?"*

Red Bull Old-Fashioned – *"A little caffeine with your classic cocktail?"*

White Claw and Milk – *"I don't even know where to begin with this one."*

Baileys and Sprite – *"Shockingly it didn't curdle."*

Aperol and Pickle Juice – *"The new pickleback?"*

Cabernet with Sprite and Rum – *"Please share this recipe with any wine connoisseur you know."*

Aperol Spritz Topped with Four Loko – *"You're probably blacking out tonight."*

Fireball Bloody Mary – *"Does this make it a spicy Bloody Mary?."*

Screwball in a Manhattan – *"No ... just no."*

Coffee Mixed with Bud Light – *"That's a unique pick-me-up."*

MOST ENTERTANING PICK-UP LINES I have received

"That shaker's not the only thing I want to see you handle with both hands." – *"Ummmm ... alrighty then."*

"This drinks not the only thing going down smooth tonight if you play your cards right." – *"How do I play my cards wrong ... ?"*

"You that smooth on the clock, or should I wait 'til you're off for the real show?" – *"Sir, when I get off the clock I will either contemplate my life choices, eat ice cream, or go to bed."*

"I just got our of jail, you wanna be the reason I go back?" – *"... slightly terrifying!"*

"Are you on the menu... because I'd love to take a long sip of you." – *"From a woman old enough to be my mother!"*

 "Honey if you keep smiling like that this drink isn't gonna be the only mistake I make tonight." – *"I somehow doubt that is true ..."*

 "You free later, or do you only shake things behind the bar?" – *"Madame, my rate doubles after last call."*

 "Honey you just worry about pouring the drinks and leave the flirting to me." – *"Makes my job a lot easier."*

 "You free after your shift, or should I fake a bar fight to get you off early?" – *"Honestly that would be pretty entertaining."*

 "That bottles not the only thing I want to see you pop tonight." – *"I didn't know how to respond to this then ... and still don't know now."*

Half the fun of mixology is that there's always new ideas and recipes emerging. Everyone has their own unique ideas that push what the definition of a drink can be and it's so inspiring. The next few pages are meant to perpetuate that. I challenge you to come up with 2 of your own original mocktails and share them with me on my social media. I can't wait to see what you all come up with!

Today we will be making a...

DIRECTIONS:

INGREDIENTS:

Tag me on Instagram with your unique creation! @the_teenage_bartender

Today we will be making a...

DIRECTIONS:

INGREDIENTS:

Tag me on Instagram with your unique creation! @the_teenage_bartender

Today we will be making a...

DIRECTIONS:

INGREDIENTS:

Tag me on Instagram with your unique creation! @the_teenage_bartender

Today we will be making a...

DIRECTIONS:

INGREDIENTS:

Tag me on Instagram with your unique creation! @the_teenage_bartender

Today we will be making a...

DIRECTIONS:

INGREDIENTS:

Tag me on Instagram with your unique creation! @the_teenage_bartender

Jack Tindle, a.k.a. The Teenage Bartender, is proud to call West Michigan his home and has been mixing up creative and tasty mocktails since he was 16 years old. He has written two mocktail recipe books while attending school and bartending at various establishments.

Come join the Teenage Bartender in his mocktail-making adventures on:

TikTok: The_Teenage_Bartender

Instagram: @the_teenage_bartender

Website: www.jacktindle.com

Shopify: www.theteenagebartender.com

photo credit:
Natalia Mae Photography

Top off your mocktail drink-making book collection by grabbing a copy of the first Teenage Bartender Mocktail Guide through The Teenage Bartender website, Amazon, or booksellers worldwide. Cheers!

www.ingramcontent.com/pod-product-compliance
Lightning Source LLC
Chambersburg PA
CBRC091205010526
44107CB00021B/1246